"Why Do I Keep Doing That?"

"Why Do I Keep Doing That?"

How to Free Yourself from the Bondage of Self-Destructive Emotions and Behaviors

Dr. Todd

Disclaimer

The information in this book is intended for educational use only. It is not intended to treat mental illness or take the place of professional mental health care. If you are having severe emotional difficulty or have recently entertained thoughts of suicide, please seek professional help immediately.

Center Path Publishing
14859 Embry Path
Apple Valley, MN 55124

Copyright © 2003 by Dr. Todd

All rights reserved. No part of this book may be used or reproduced in any manner whatsoever without written permission from the publisher, except in the case of brief quotations in critical articles or reviews.

Library of Congress Control Number: 2002093796

ISBN 0-9724022-0-9

Printed in the United States of America

∞ The paper used in this publication meets the minimum requirements of the American National Standard for Information Sciences - Permanence of Paper for Printed Library Materials, ANSI Z39.48-1984.

Order Information:

A quantity discount of this title is available from Center Path Publishing. Inquiries should be sent via e-mail to: orders@centerpathpublishing.com

Visit us on-line at:
www.centerpathpublishing.com

This book is dedicated to my wife, Monique

*" Awaken you dreamers
asleep in your beds.
Balloons and streamers
decorate the inside of your heads.
Please let some out.
Do it today.
And don't let the loveless ones
sell you a world wrapped in grey."*

- Andy Partridge, XTC

Dr. Todd's Story

~~~~~~~~~~

    I'm not exactly sure what was in the bottle of fluid that I had been sniffing all day - something that smelled like a cross between garlic and gasoline. The solution sloshed against the sides of the brown glass jug as I drew the mouth of the bottle to just under my nose and inhaled. The sound of the rushing air reverberated in the bottle like the sound of the ocean in a large seashell. A tingling wave slithered up my chest to the top of my head and down the tops of my arms. For a brief moment time stood still. I no longer felt angry. I no longer felt sad. But most of all, I no longer felt isolated and alone.

    As my eyes began to refocus, I saw a young woman on TV standing on the third story window ledge of a large brick house. She was tall, with long wavy dark brown hair which blew lazily in the breeze to expose the thick rope of hemp she had tightened around her neck. "Look at me Damien! It's all for you!" she exclaimed with joy as she stepped from the ledge. The family who was gathered for a party outside of the house watched in horror as the girl's body dropped, snatched to a halt by the tightening of the rope and jerked back through the second story windows, shattering them as her body catapulted through. "Go Satan!" I shouted as I leapt up from my chair and thrust my fist in the air. Then all went black.

I woke up several minutes later face down in a soggy patch of drool-soaked carpet. As I came to, I could hear the voices on the television once again. This was the third time I had watched The Omen that day and I could tell by what was happening in the movie that I hadn't been out long. I worked my way back onto my feet and plopped down onto the big pillows of the loveseat that my father had made out of some plywood and brown automotive carpet.

My left forearm was aching. I looked down to see how much blood there was and felt quite disappointed that the "666" I had cut into it earlier was not more prominent. The skin had only been scratched. I fumbled around a bit in an effort to find the razor blade I had used, but I was unable to find it. "Where the hell did it go!"

I tried to act frustrated at my inability to find the blade, but deep down, I was relieved. I hated pain. I already had endured so much of it. I hadn't cut my arm deeper to begin with because it just hurt too much. But I certainly couldn't admit that to myself. After all, I was bad! I was mean and tough!

As The Omen continued to unfold before me on the TV screen, a feeling of urgency began to swell within me. The longer I sat there, the more powerful this feeling became. I started to feel like there was something that I needed to do or somewhere that I needed to go; almost like I was running late for something. But there was nowhere I was supposed to be and nothing I was supposed to do. It felt like something was pulling and tugging at my insides. I knew I had to do something but what? My palms began to sweat and my head was racing. "Fine!" I said. I grabbed a socket wrench and dashed out to my car.

Gravel and dust ground into my bare knees as I knelt down and slid my torso under the driver's seat of the car. The first nut loosened easily.

The second nut was a bit rusty, but I was able to get it loose. To get to the other two, I had to go around to the other side of the car. The third and fourth nuts came off surprisingly well. I was shocked. This was good! I brushed myself off as I climbed out of the car. I stood there for a moment and reveled in a job well done. Already my emotions had started to settle down. The panic I had felt just a few minutes ago had left and had been replaced with a feeling of pride and satisfaction. Now to really make the afternoon worthwhile, the job just needed to be completed.

I leaned back into the car, and in a moment of sheer excitement, pulled the unbolted front bench seat out of my car. Clouds of dust kicked up as I dragged the seat over to toward the dumpster, and with one Herculean effort, flipped it inside. I could now go back into the apartment and watch The Omen in peace.

For the following year and a half, I drove around in a car without any front seats. I just sat on an upside-down milk crate. I felt resentful that other people had nicer cars than I did. But I never made the connection that it was my action that was responsible for my car's pathetic condition. It was me who pulled out the front seats and threw them away. It was me who stabbed the scissors through the dashboard. It was me who pulled off the rear-view mirrors. It was me who cut out the rear wheel wells with a hack saw (just in case I got 'mag wheels' some day). Yes, they were my actions; and my actions were responsible for my car's condition.

My car was really a microcosm of my entire life. Everything was messed up. Each day brought another stream of bad decisions, frustration and unhappiness. I once stole a friend's stereo so that I could sell it to buy drugs. I broke into a friend's home when he was out of town and held a huge party - literally trashing his house. I would impulsively smash things, steal things, buy things I couldn't afford, yell at people, not show up for work (when I had a job), or suddenly become belligerent and obnoxious toward those who tried to care for me. I was always shocked when people became angry with me. I was even more shocked when people retaliated against me. I felt like I was always the victim; not them.

By the time I was 19 years old, I found myself living in an abandoned house. I was functionally illiterate and had difficulty carrying on an intelligent conversation with anyone. I had nothing and could do nothing. I was profoundly depressed and suicidal. I felt like no matter what I did, no matter what I tried, and no matter what goals I set, they only served to dig me further and further into a pit of despair from which escape seemed impossible. I wanted to free myself from these self-destructive emotions and behaviors, but I had no idea how.

I could not figure out why some people were so happy, when I was so miserable; why some people were so successful in everything that they did, when I couldn't seem to make anything work; why other people had so many friends and people who cared about them very much, while I suffered in isolation. I couldn't figure out why the world had singled me out as one of its outcast and despised. But then one day in early September, 1983, everything began to change.

It was about 1:30 in the morning on September 10th. I was standing in the kitchen of the abandoned house staring blankly out of the window at the woods which served to shelter the house from the sight of the cars driving on Highway 33. Ohio was experiencing another Indian summer, which was very good because there was no heat in the house. A warm breeze drizzled in through the window, making the room quite comfortable. Without any warning, I suddenly felt my body freeze in place. A wave of warm tingling energy, rushed into every corner of my body, and I was filled with a feeling of calm. I looked around the room and everything looked different - clearer. All around me I heard a deep comforting voice say "you don't have to live like this anymore."

Although I didn't realize it at the time, this moment marked an end to my tortured life; a life which had been nothing, meant nothing and was going nowhere, and a beginning of a new life which would be filled with passion, joy and excitement far beyond anything I could have ever dreamed. But this did not come easily.

When I began to rebuild my life from its shattered state, I had nothing to call my own but the jumbled shards of emotion which hijacked my daily thoughts with deep-seated despair, hopelessness, depression, loneliness and fear. For years, I fought a losing battle with depression and anxiety while going from psychologist to psychiatrist, taking lithium, Prozac or Ritalin; anything to stop my head from racing and to numb the discomfort of the intense emotions which I could not understand. I used to jokingly call my condition "spastic brain syndrome," but my thinly veiled humor offered me little comfort.

For many years, I was a slave to the negative emotions of stress, anxiety, worthlessness and fear. They permeated every corner of my life. My world seemed chaotic and out of control. I ran from one meaningless job to another and from one relationship to another, trying to find peace and happiness. But everywhere I went and everything that I tried was undermined by my self-destructive behaviors. I wouldn't show up for meetings, I would act rude to my friends, I would jump from project to project, starting things and not finishing them, and I would sit and wallow in my depression and self-pity for weeks at a time. The tragedy was that I hated living that way. I hated feeling bad all of the time. I hated watching my relationships disintegrate before my eyes while I sat by and watched powerlessly. I hated not being able to accomplish anything. I hated not being able to understand what I was feeling, let alone to be able to communicate my feelings with someone else.

Throughout this whole time of hardship and struggle, there was one thing I did right. That was to make commitment to myself that I would maintain a willingness to take whatever action was necessary, no matter how extreme or uncomfortable, in order to improve my life. I knew that I could not just wish my life to be better, or I would have been happy long ago. It would take a sustained purposeful effort on my part to make it better. The problem was that I had no clue what that effort should be.

I dove into twelve-step programs, religion, self-help books, audio programs and higher education with all of the intensity I could muster – and I learned a lot. Unfortunately, that information had only limited affect on how I felt. Even after years of learning theories of why I was so unhappy and developing an extensive reperatoire of catchy sayings, I still felt a lot of fear, anxiety and depression. It was not that the information was useless. On the contrary, the knowledge I acquired was helpful in understanding *some* of what was going on with me. Unfortunately, self-knowledge only took me so far.

It wasn't until I learned how to change my emotions through very specific action that my life really started to turn around. It wasn't until I applied the techniques I describe in this book that I was truly able to free myself from the bondage of negative emotions and create a life that was filled with passion, fulfillment and meaning. I have made it my life's mission to distill the essence of how emotions are experienced, how they manifest themselves in our lives and how to change them.

Mastering your emotions is the single most important skill you can develop in life. Once you learn the techniques to free yourself from the bondage of self-destructive emotions and behaviors, your life will become filled with happiness and meaning. No matter how rich or poor you are, regardless of what career you choose, how big your house is, what kind of car you drive, or how extravagant or modest your lifestyle, you can create a high quality of life if you are willing to work through the simple steps outlined in this book.

What This Book Will Do For You

~~~~~~~~~~~~~~~~

If you experience negative emotions such as anxiety, fear, stress and depression and you want to stop feeling that way, this book is for you. If you repeatedly find yourself in one unhealthy relationship after another and you want to figure out why you keep ending up in those relationships, this book is for you. If you indulge in self-destructive behaviors, such as addictions or compulsions, and you want to learn how to stop doing them, this book is for you. If you react too much to the actions of other people at work or in relationships and you want to stop reacting so much, this book is for you. If you want to finally take control over your emotions, rather than having them take control over you, this book is for you.

In this book, you will learn a simple, but powerful, model to help you understand how your mind works, what drives you to do the things that you do, why you feel the way you feel and how to change what you feel and how you act.

By the time you finish this book, you should:

- understand how emotions are created and how these emotions can impact your life;
- understand why your emotional intensity may be more than other people's;
- understand how negative emotions drive you to act in ways that make you unhappy;
- understand how your memories can impact your mood;
- understand how your emotions affect your decisions;
- understand how to overcome the destructive influence of negative emotions.

The Three Keys to Getting the Most Out of This Book

This book is designed to teach you how to *change* your emotions, in addition to teaching you *about* your emotions. You can learn all you need to know about your emotions just by reading through the text. But to actually *change* your emotions, that's a whole different issue. Change requires three things from you: a willingness to take some action, the courage to feel a bit disoriented while you go through change, and the strength to not take yourself too seriously.

The Willingness to Take Action

If you are willing to take a little bit of action on a daily basis, you can create huge change in your life. The key is the willingness. It doesn't matter whether you want to take the action or not, or whether you think the action is silly or not. All that matters is that you are willing to take action; to do something.

Just as you cannot read a book on weightlifting and suddenly have the body of an underwear model, it is impossible to exchange all of the negative emotions in your life with positive ones without doing something. You can build a positive emotional state just like you can build biceps, but it requires you to show up and exercise a little bit every day. You don't have to do the exercises perfectly, it doesn't even matter if there are times where you don't want to do them at all, but if you just work through the exercises laid out in this book, you will change.

The Courage to Feel Disoriented

When you live with a negative emotion or a self-destructive behavior for a long time, it becomes part of your identity. You become used to living that way. In order to remove a negative emotion or behavior, you really have to recreate your identity. This is not easy. Any time you go through a significant change in life, you will experience a strange sense of disorientation as you cut loose the anchor of habit.

Many people are gung-ho and have a willingness to take action at first. But once they begin to change, the emotional volatility and uncertainty they experience frightens them and they stop taking action, and before long, they relapse into their old way of living. But it doesn't have to be that way for you.

Changing your life is kind of like cleaning out a closet. Half-way through the process, stuff is laying everywhere and the closet looks worse than it did before you started. But if you keep working at it, pretty soon your closet looks a lot better than it did before. You have to expect to feel a bit uneasy, disoriented and emotionally messy. You may feel happy one minute, fearful the next, anxious the next, then happy again, then a bit confused; like your emotions are wandering around aimlessly. If you can muster the courage to continue taking action through this emotional disorientation, you will be successful.

The Strength to Not Take Yourself too Seriously

When it comes to changing your life, it is important that you be able to develop a sense of humor. The more you can laugh at your insanity, the more your mind will be willing to change. Here's why:

Your mind will automatically retreat from things it perceives to be a threat. On the other hand, it will tend to latch on to those things which it perceives to be supportive. If you take the approach that you are bad, that your behavior is bad, that your emotions are bad, your mind will retreat from dealing with it. Your mind will rebel because it will associate your focus on change with a poor image of yourself. If you beat yourself up as a way to motivate yourself to change – change won't happen.

Instead, you need to leap up in the morning and embrace your insanity. Learn to find humor in the ridiculous things you think and do. This is not to say you don't take them seriously, only that you don't beat yourself up about them. The more you can laugh at the absurdity of how you act at times, the more you mind will be willing to spend time attempting to change. Just give yourself a break, don't take yourself too seriously, and find some humor in how you behave and feel. You will be doing yourself a huge service in hastening your progress into a better quality of life.

It's All About Changing Emotions

By changing your emotions, you can improve just about any aspect of your life. Whether you want to improve the intimacy and communication in your personal relationships, improve how you feel about yourself, or even improve your effectiveness in your career, it all starts with your emotions. By purchasing this book you have taken an important first step. I urge you to work through the exercises and take many more steps down the path toward a happier and more fulfilling life.

Acknowledgements

I would like first and foremost like to thank you for purchasing this book. All of the effort poured into creating this book would be for naught, if you did not read it. I would like to thank my wife, Monique. Words fail to describe the deep level of love and gratitude I hold for her. I would like to thank Doug Steindorf for his remarkable committment to teaching me how to live a spiritual life, and the family of John Reinhart for taking me in when I had no place to live. I would like to thank all of the people of the National Speakers Association in Minnesota for their guidance and support; especially my friend Robin Getman who talked me out of taking voice lessons. I would like to thank Candia Lea Cole for her encouragement and support when I first embarked on this project several years ago. I would like to thank my editor Jean Marie Stine for helping me develop a manuscript that had a point. Finally, I would like to thank the staff at the Barnes & Noble in Eagan, Minnesota, for allowing me to take over a corner in their cafe for the last year and a half while I wrote this book.

Thanks Everyone!

Table of Contents

Dr. Todd's Story		ix
What This Book Will Do For You		xv
Acknowledgements		xxi
Introduction:	Why Do I Keep Doing That?	1
Exercise:	How Do Emotions Affect Me?	15
Chapter 1:	Your Perceptions and Emotions	19
Exercise:	Developing Emotional Awareness	51
Chapter 2:	Sensitivity and Emotional Intensity	57
Exercise:	What Is Your Sensitivity Temperament?	67
Chapter 3:	The Emotional Memory Loop	73
Exercise:	Automatic Thoughts and Phantom Events	95
Chapter 4:	Three Facts, Eight Realities and Four Techniques of Change	101
Exercise:	The Daily Perception Diary	119
Glossary		151
Index		157

Introduction

"Why Do I Keep Doing That?"

~~~~~~~~~~~~~~~~

It was around 9:00 p.m. on a Friday night when a very well-dressed couple was seated at one of my tables. They both looked to be in their early 30s and I could tell by the way they were interacting with each other, that they had just started dating. The woman was tall and thin with wavy sandy-blonde hair and wore a long black evening gown. The gentleman was lean, tan and athletic, and was wearing a nice suit.

I always liked waiting on couples who were dating because they were usually on their best behavior and they almost always tipped well. This couple seemed no different. They were both polite, smiling and cracking the occasional bad joke. The mood was very light and happy – that was, until I delivered a cheddar fondue to the table.

Somehow in the bustle of a busy Friday night, I had misunderstood that the woman wanted a cheddar fondue, when in fact she actually wanted a Swiss fondue. I apologized for the mix up, told her that it would be two or three minutes for me to bring a Swiss fondue out for her and offered her a free dessert.

She suddenly became horribly upset and belligerent. Every table in the room watched in amazement as the woman's tirade unfolded. She picked up pieces of her bread and threw them back down onto the table like a three-year-old in the clutches of a temper tantrum. She refused to respond to me – or even look at me – and was trembling with anger. She was inconsolable. I could see from the shocked look on her date's face that her sudden outburst scared him to death.

Within a few minutes I brought out a Swiss fondue to the table and the gentleman thanked me and apologized for his date's behavior. For the rest of the evening, the two of them didn't speak. They just sat there quietly and stared down at their food. When they were done, I delivered the bill. The gentleman quickly paid and the two of them quietly left.

I really felt bad for the couple in the restaurant, but I felt especially bad for the woman because I understood first-hand what she was going through. I knew that her uncontrollable outburst likely meant that she would be alone again, sifting through the personal ads to find a new date and mentally whipping herself for acting so obnoxiously. Her problem was that she was caught in the bondage of negative emotions, which at times became so intense that they drove her to act in a self-destructive way.

Everyone, at one time or another, has experienced times when emotions have driven them to act in ways which they later regret. Although you may not have become upset over a cheddar fondue, there are probably many other situations about which you feel very angry, depressed, anxious, stressed, fearful or desperate. The more you experience these negative feelings, the more they sap the happiness, success and quality out of your life.

In this book you will learn how to free yourself from the bondage of self-destructive emotions and behaviors by understanding how your emotions are created, how they affect you and how you can change them. The first chapter describes your emotions and how they are created. Next you will be introduced to the concept of emotional sensitivity, which refers to the intensity with which you tend to experience your emotions and about emotional hijackings. Emotional hijackings occur when emotions become so overwhelming that they overpower your ability to control how you feel and act. We will then shift gears a bit and discuss the concept of emotional memory and how your emotional memories create your mood, affect your decision-making, and create the automatic thoughts which run through your mind during the day. The next chapter will describe several facts and techniques you can apply in your life right away to free yourself from the bondage of self-destructive emotions and behaviors. The last chapter will teach you how to keep an emotional action diary to help you improve your quality of life.

This introduction describes each of these concepts briefly to give you an overview of the entire model presented here. Let's start out by describing what emotions are and why you have them.

Positive and Negative Emotions

There are two major types of emotions which are created in two different emotional centers in the brain: positive emotions and negative emotions. Although both positive and negative emotions are important to help you survive, they do it in opposite ways. Positive emotions help to ensure your survival by motivating you to explore, form relationships and support a social structure. As long as you don't perceive an imminent threat to your life or well-being, positive emotions will predominate. Positive emotions drive *proactive* behaviors.

Your Eight Primary Emotions

Positive Emotions	Negative Emotions
Joy	Worthlessness
Empowerment	Anxiety
Confidence	Stress
Attraction	Fear

However, if you perceive that something is threatening you, negative emotions take over. Negative emotions are designed to make you withdraw, fight or try to escape from situations which you perceive to be harmful to you. In this way, negative emotions are also important survival tools just like positive emotions. Because negative emotions are designed to help you cope with a threat which is more imminent, they will be more powerful in their influence over your actions than positive emotions. Consequently, strong negative emotions have the potential to hijack your behavior and drive you to act in self-destructive ways. Negative emotions drive *reactive* behaviors.

Your Perceptions Drive Your Emotions

In the first chapter, you will learn about subconscious perceptions and how they are responsible for creating your emotions. It turns out that whenever you respond emotionally to something that happens to you or around you it is because your subconscious mind saw something in the event which had meaning for you. More specifically, it had meaning about your value or effectiveness as a human being, or it had meaning about how hostile or unpredictable your world was. For example, if somebody was disrespectful to you by saying something malicious behind your back, you would respond emotionally. You would respond because their actions would mean something to you about your value as an individual. If you feel overwhelmed by a project at work or you feel anxiety about going out on stage to give a presentation, it is because at the subconscious level, you feel that you will be ineffective. If someone threatens you with a knife, you will respond because you will perceive hostility. If you have to change jobs, you will experience the emotion of stress because your life is no longer as predictable as it was. No matter what the situation is that you face, if you respond emotionally, it is because subconsciously you saw meaning in the event.

Primary and Secondary Emotions

In addition to having positive and negative emotions, you also have what are called primary and secondary emotions. Primary emotions are those which are an immediate reaction to an event. There are a total of eight primary emotions; four positive primary emotions and four negative primary emotions. Your positive primary emotions are joy, confidence, empowerment and attraction, and your negative primary emotions are worthlessness, stress, anxiety and fear.

A secondary emotion is one which you experience a few moments after experiencing a primary emotion. Secondary emotions are an amalgam of your conscious thoughts about the event coupled with the mixture of primary emotions. Unlike primary emotions, there is no set number of secondary emotions. Some of the most common secondary emotions you may experience are anger, desperation, apathy or rage.

To illustrate the difference between primary and secondary emotions, imagine that you are driving through an intersection where the light is green and someone driving on the cross-street runs their red light and almost hits you. The very first emotion you will experience will be fear because your subconscious mind perceives a major threat to your safety. But within a few moments, that fear may turn into anger when you think about what just happened. Fear is the primary emotion and anger is the secondary emotion. You will only experience the secondary emotion if you experience a primary one first. There is much more on primary and secondary emotions in the next chapter.

Sensitivity and Emotional Intensity

How much influence emotions have over your behavior depends on how intensely you experience those emotions. If you are a person who experiences emotions very intensely, your emotions will have a greater impact on your life than someone who doesn't experience emotions very much at all. Whether you experience emotions intensely or not depends on your emotional sensitivity.

Your emotional sensitivity is like an emotional volume knob which is hard-wired in your brain by the time you are three or four years old. Once your emotional volume knob is set, it doesn't change to any significant degree throughout your life.

If you are someone who doesn't experience emotions very intensely at all, you have what is called a low-sensitivity temperament. If you have a low-sensitivity temperament, you will be much less influenced by your emotions when you make decisions and, because you don't rely on how you feel to determine your actions, you will find it much easier to be disciplined. Low-sensitivity people are well suited for occupations and hobbies which are by their nature hard, fast and intense, such as law enforcement, fire fighting and professional sports.

If you are someone who experiences emotions very intensely, you have what is called a high-sensitivity temperament. A high-sensitivity temperament means that you will experience everything more intensely. In addition to feeling emotions more intensely, sounds may be more piercing, colors brighter, your sense of touch more acute and odors may smell stronger. In just about every respect, you are more susceptible to stimuli from your environment. Because of this, you will tend to make decisions and act based on how you feel at the moment, and you will find it harder to be disciplined. High-sensitivity people are well suited for occupations and hobbies which require a great deal of observation, intuition and creativity, such as writing, art, advertising and acting.

Somewhere between the two extremes of high-sensitivity and a low-sensitivity lies most of the population. Most people are somewhere around the middle, with fewer people on each end of the spectrum. But those with a high-sensitivity temperament are the ones who suffer the most from intense emotions.

In a workshop that I recently presented on emotions, I asked everyone in the audience to complete a short questionnaire to measure their sensitivity. Every single person in the audience scored on the high end of the sensitivity spectrum. This makes sense because those who experience emotions more intensely will have their life impacted more by their emotions and, consequently, have a greater desire to understand them.

Emotional Hijackings

In the early 1980s I was dating a woman for whom I deeply cared, named Pam. One weekend night we went out with John; another very close friend of mine. John and Pam were two of the most genuinely kind people I knew, and I was excited about the three of us going out and having some fun. I picked both of them up and we went to go get something to eat.

Three hours later, John and Pam were sitting on the hood of my car trying to figure out what my problem was. Throughout their guarded conversation, they would occasionally glance into my car to see my face angrily glaring back at them. At one point, I grabbed my rearview mirror, jerked it free from the windshield with a loud pop and whipped it with all my might against the back seat. I can still see the puzzled looks on the faces of John and Pam as they peered in on me. I felt so enraged and overwhelmed with anger, but I had no idea why. Nothing had happened to justify the rage I experienced; I just spontaneously snapped. To this day, I have no clue what made me so upset. But this was only one event in a recurrent pattern of emotional hijackings that I would experience.

Although the example above is one of the many ways in which an emotional hijacking unfolded in my life, your experience may be quite different. If you tend to experience worthlessness, an emotional hijacking may keep you from getting out of bed for days on end. If you experience anxiety, an emotional hijacking may keep you from going to a social gathering. If you experience stress, an emotional hijacking may make you feel overwhelmed. If you experience fear, an emotional hijacking may create fits of anger. Your experience with an emotional hijacking will not necessarily be the same as someone else's experience. But in all cases, an emotional hijacking is when the negative emotions you experience become so overwhelming that you lose the ability to control your thoughts and behavior for a time – usually with negative consequences.

Emotional Memory Loops

One of the facts about the subconscious mind is that it cannot differentiate between what is actual from what is imagined. This means that you can respond emotionally just as much to something which you only imagine to be true as you can to something which is actually true. To illustrate this phenomenon, think about movies. Have you ever seen a movie that made you laugh? Have you ever seen a movie that made you cry? Have you ever seen a movie that made you angry? Movies are not real. Consciously, we know they are not real. But the subconscious mind, which is responsible for generating our emotions, cannot tell what is real and what is not. Consequently, you can react emotionally to things which are only imagined. Have you ever become upset just thinking about what someone might say to you or what might happen? Of course you have. We all have. This is just another example of how the subconscious mind cannot differentiate what is real from what is imagined.

Because your mind is always at work playing bits of conversations and various situations through your head, your emotions are constantly being stimulated by these imagined events. The content of the thoughts and the emotions which are stimulated will set your mood. If the din of thought and emotion is positive, you will feel happy and in a good mood. If the thoughts and emotions are negative, you will feel irritable and in a bad mood.

Now here is where this phenomenon gets interesting: It is actually not your thoughts which stimulate an emotional response. Rather, your subconscious perceptions stimulate mild emotional responses to the events you encounter throughout the day. These small emotional responses then recall *emotional memories* and the emotional memories create the thoughts that go through your mind.

Here is the process by which this happens: An emotional memory is stored in our mind whenever we experience a strong emotional event; for example, if we witness a crime. The memory is stored in two parts. One part is the factual portion of the memory – the details of what actually happened. This factual memory is stored in the conscious mind. The second part of the memory is the emotional content – how you felt when the event occurred. This emotional memory is stored in the subconscious mind.

The conscious mind does not store information nearly as well as the subconscious mind. Consequently, many of the factual details surrounding an event may be lost over time, but the emotions experienced during the event remain intact. When that emotional memory is recalled, the emotion of the earlier event pops back, even though the details may be fuzzy at best. It turns out that our conscious mind dislikes things which are incomplete or ambiguous, so it will set out to "fill in" the missing information with facts that it "thinks" are consistent with the emotional component of the memory. Whew! Got all that? Let's take a look at an example.

For many years eyewitness testimony was considered to be the most reliable form of testimony. After all, it was thought that the witness who actually saw the crime happen should know the facts of the case, right? Well, research has shown that in as little as a few days, eyewitness testimony becomes less and less reliable as the facts of what actually happened begin to fade. Six months to a year later, many of the details of the crime have been forgotten. When the eyewitness takes the stand and is asked to recall the events in question, they will be recalling the strong emotional portion of the memory and a bunch of fuzzy details. Because the mind likes to have consistency and dislikes ambiguity, those fuzzy details will be re-arranged, changed and filled in to make the conscious memory consistent with the emotion. Although many of the 'facts' that the eyewitness will recall are not true, they will feel as though they are true to the witness.

So why is all this important for you to know? As you go through your day, you are constantly experiencing events. To each of these events you have an emotional reaction, even if only mildly. Each time you have an emotional reaction, your subconscious searches through its memory banks to pull up other memories that have a similar emotional content. The recalled emotional memory will also pull what's left of the factual information of the event into your conscious mind. Since many of the facts may no longer be there, your conscious mind creates images, bits of conversation or other details which are consistent with the theme of the emotion. The mixture of recalled details and synthesized details are displayed in your thoughts while you experience the emotional part of the memory.

Now, remember a few paragraphs ago when you learned that your subconscious mind cannot differentiate that which is actual from that which is imagined? Well, the emotional memory which you recalled, along with the partially factual thoughts which ran through your head, stimulates the emotional centers as though it was a new event. This is how your perceptions become self-reinforcing.

Let's step through this process one more time: When you experience an event, your perceptions stimulate an emotional response. That emotion will trigger the recall of emotional memories that are similar in nature. Those emotional memories are then re-experienced just like they were actual events and the emotional reaction to those memories causes yet another similar emotional memory to be pulled up from the subconscious; and so the cycle continues.

Self-Fulfilling Prophecies

Self-fulfilling prophecy is where what you subconsciously perceive to be true is what will actually manifest in your life. If you have a low perception of value, you will make decisions which will reinforce that perception. If you have the perception that the world is a hostile place, you will create hostility around you. If you have the perception that the world is chaotic and unpredictable, you will do things which create turmoil in your life. If you have the perception that you are powerless and have no control over your environment, you will tend to put yourself in situations where you are powerless and have no control. Why?

When you are faced with a situation and have a decision to make, you will tend to make the decision that feels right to you. Since you rely on your emotions to make decisions, you are ultimately relying on the condition of your perceptions to make the decision. Since your perceptions reflect your assessment of yourself and the world around you, when you make a decision based on how you feel, it will be consistent with your perceptions. Consequently, your perceptions become the basis of a self-fulfilling prophecy.

For example, a woman I know grew up in an environment where she was abused emotionally and physically as a child. Because of this, her perception was that she was not valued, that people were hostile and that she was powerless to do anything about it. Although she didn't consciously seek out abusive partners, her current abusive marriage was merely the latest in a string of abusive relationships. For reasons she couldn't explain, she kept accepting dates from men who were abusive, rather than going out with men who were kind and supportive.

Those who have gone from job to job, relationship to relationship, or city to city in an effort to escape from bad situations, only to find themselves in the same situation again and again, have experienced first-hand how frustrating self-fulfilling prophecies can be. There is an old saying that no matter where you run; there you are. Although you can change your environment, if you don't change the subconscious perceptions which created your problems in the first place, you will quickly find yourself back in the same mess again.

Free Yourself from the Bondage

The key to freeing yourself from the emotional hijackings, the negative emotional memories and the destructive self-fulfilling prophesies is simply to change your subconscious perceptions. But this is not necessarily as easy as it sounds for several reasons:

- You will often times have to take action which is inconsistent with your current perceptions. Even though your new behaviors may be much healthier than your old behaviors, the feelings you experience may be uncomfortable, and your subconscious mind will try to steer you back to your old way of acting.
- You will have to always keep in mind that what you feel is real, often times is not. You cannot take your emotions too seriously. There is a temptation to trust what you feel, especially when your emotions are intense. Fighting this temptation is often times difficult.
- Changing your perceptions involves applying a little bit of pressure every day through action. Your perceptions developed by experiencing events, and they can only change by experiencing events. Your thoughts cannot change your perceptions, only daily action will.

In spite of the challenges posed by changing your perceptions, I can tell you from personal experience that it is entirely possible for you to do it. All you have to do is be willing to take the necessary action to make the changes happen.

Why Do I Keep Doing That?

In this introductory chapter, you were introduced to important concepts about emotions and the kind of impact they can have on your life. You learned that you have eight primary emotions and about how they are important survival mechanisms. There was a quick introduction to the concept of emotional sensitivity and how that relates to the intensity with which you experience your emotions. You read about how emotions can be so overwhelming that they hijack your behavior and drive you to act in ways which are self-destructive. The concept of emotional memory was discussed, and how that relates to self-fulfilling prophesies. Finally, you read that the key to changing your emotions and creating a better quality of life depends on changing your subconscious perceptions, and that changing your perceptions can be quite a challenge.

Until now, few people have been successful in truly recreating their lives. This is because most people have not considered the effects, or even the existence, of the subconscious mind and the perceptions it holds. The book you have in your hands describes for the first time how your subconscious perceptions drive your behavior and finally answers the question: "Why do I keep doing that?"

A Final Note on the Importance of Exercise

Most people would agree that you cannot build a better body merely by reading a diet book or watching a work-out video. You cannot renovate your home by reading architectural magazines and watching home improvement shows on television. Hardly anything can be changed merely by *knowing* something. We must *do* something. To build our physical health, we need to do physical exercise. To build better mental and emotional health, we need to do mental and emotional exercise. At the end of each chapter, there are exercises to do. If you do the exercises, you will change much more than if you don't. The more effort that you put in, the more things will change for you.

Exercise

How Do Emotions Affect Me?

There was a time in my life when I bragged about the fact that I did not have any emotions at all. Boy was I wrong! The fact was that my emotions were so intense, jumbled up and confusing that I did my best to just repress the whole mess. One of the major challenges I faced when I began changing my life was trying to figure out what I was feeling. I can remember many long talks with my wife, Monique, where I was just trying to figure out what I was feeling. The problem was that until I knew what I was feeling, there was no way to do anything about it.

The next few exercises are designed to improve your emotional awareness. This first exercise is very simple. It is designed to get you thinking about what emotions you feel and how they tend to affect you. Although this is an easy exercise, don't skip it. Every exercise is important.

Where Do You See Yourself?

There are four lines below; one for each of your subconscious perceptions. The bold word above the line is the subconscious perception that is responsible for creating the two emotions listed at each end below the line. All of the emotions on the right hand side are positive emotions, all of the emotions on the left are negative ones.

On each of the lines below place an "X" where you see youself between the two emotional extremes. For example, if you feel depressed a lot and you feel that you don't have a very high self-esteem, you may mark the line like this:

Value

———X————————————————————
Worthlessness   Joy

Value

————————————————————————
Worthlessness   Joy

Effectiveness

————————————————————————
Anxiety   Empowerment

Predictability

————————————————————————
Stress   Confidence

Hostility

————————————————————————
Fear   Attraction

Give an Example of a Negative Emotion

Of the four negative emotions listed on the opposite page, write a specific example of how one of those emotions affected your life. Did you not go to a party because of your anxiety? Have you changed your routine because of fear? Pick one negative emotion and write down how that emotion affected your behavior. Don't just write down the situation where you felt the emotion. It is important to describe how the emotion affected your behavior.

_____

_____

_____

_____

_____

_____

_____

_____

_____

Give an Example of a Positive Emotion

Of the four positive emotions listed, write a specific example of how one of those emotions affected your life. Did you take on a project at work because you felt empowered? How did you act toward those around you during a joyful time? Even if all of your emotions are on the negative side of the scale, pick the most positive one and write an example when you felt that positive emotion. Again, don't just describe the situation, but describe how you acted when you felt the emotion.

_____

_____

_____

_____

_____

_____

_____

_____

_____

Chapter 1

Your Perceptions and Emotions

"I Hate Myself and I Want To Die" was the title of the song that Kurt Cobain, the singer and songwriter from the grunge rock band *Nirvana*, contributed to *The Beavis and Butthead Experience* LP. A few months later, Kurt injected himself with a deadly dose of heroin and pointed a Remington 20 gauge shotgun at his face.

The room was a gruesome site when his disfigured body was found three days later in the garage apartment attached to his home. Blood, hair and pieces of skull which where once part a creative genius were strewn about, laying dried out and lifeless. On the floor next to his body lay his driver's license and a hand-written suicide note neatly arranged.

The world was shocked. Kurt seemed to have everything - success, money, fame and thousands, if not millions, of admirers all over the world. But what Kurt lacked was happiness. His successes felt empty. His heavy drug use only intensified his feelings of self-hatred and disdain for those around him. The overwhelming negative emotions were more than Kurt could handle. In spite of having all of the success and material wealth imaginable, he decided to end his life.

On the other side of the world, the spiritual leader of Tibetan Buddhism His Holiness the Dalai Lama begins another day in exile. Since his escape from the Chinese invasion of Tibet in 1950, he has witnessed the genocide of more than 1.2 million innocent Tibetans at the hands of the Chinese - one-fifth of the entire population. Thousands of immense and beautiful monasteries, such as Samye, built over a thousand years ago, are all pummeled into ruin.

The Dalai Lama lives under very simple conditions. Yet the Dalai Lama beams with joy and fulfillment. In spite of the difficulties he has had to endure, he is passionately committed a philosophy of love, self-sacrifice, tolerance and non-violence. He travels the world to spread his philosophy of happy and ethical living. The Dalai Lama was awarded the Nobel Peace Prize in 1989 for his spiritual efforts and is regarded by many to be one of the most charismatic and important spiritual figures alive today.

While Kurt Cobain had fame and fortune, he also suffered from intense negative emotions which destroyed any chance of happiness and meaning he could have found in his life. In contrast, even though the Dalai Lama lives in exile, his life is wonderfully fulfilling and meaningful. The difference between Kurt Cobain and His Holiness the Dalai Lama is merely a difference of whether they experienced predominantly negative or positive emotions.

In this chapter, you will discover what emotions are and why you have them. You will learn how emotions are created by the two emotional centers in your brain and how positive emotions and negative emotions differ from each other in many important ways. This will be followed by a discussion of your eight primary emotions of anxiety, stress, worthlessness, fear, joy, confidence, attraction and empowerment, as well as your negative secondary emotions of anger, desperation, withdrawal, disappointment, apathy and guarding. Finally, you will understand how emotions create the way in which you interact with the world around you. If you are emotionally healthy, you will tend to be much more successful, more fulfilled and your life will have more meaning than if you experience a daily pattern of negative emotions.

Emotions are Powerful Survival Mechanisms

The word emotion comes from the Latin words *emovere*, which means to *stir up*, and *motio*, which means *to move*; and that's exactly what emotions do - they stir you up and move you. But, they don't just stir you up and move you randomly. They do so for a very specific reason: *your survival*. When you first arrived in this world, there were four basic questions important to your survival that you had to answer as quickly as possible:

- How important am I to the people around me?
- How much control do I have over myself and the world around me?
- How predictable or chaotic is my world?
- How hostile or nurturing is my world?

Based on your early experiences, these questions were answered by the time you were three or four years old. These early childhood experiences set up perceptions about yourself and your world and stored them in the subconscious. These perceptions, in turn, were what stimulated the emotions which made up your *emotional personality*. Your emotional personality is the combination of your general mood, how you react to different situations and how you form relationships with other people. It is important to remember that your emotional personality is designed as a survival mechanism and is defined by your perceptions about yourself and your environment. How you perceive yourself and your environment will create the way in which you respond emotionally to situations in which you find yourself. Let's take a look at each of the four questions listed above individually and see how they affect your emotional personality.

How important am I to the people around me?

During prehistoric times, if you found yourself unwanted by the group of people you lived with, you would probably find yourself living alone. In a very real sense, not having the support and security of the group meant death, for it was very unlikely that you would be able to survive very well completely on your own. Your survival was dependant on your group needing you and wanting you. Because of this, nature wired us with a need to feel valued by those around us.

Several decades ago it was discovered that if an infant did not receive a great deal of human contact immediately after birth, the infant would fail to thrive and grow. As a matter of fact, the skulls and brains of infants who were raised in orphanages did not even develop correctly if they were not held, even though they were given plenty to eat. A few orphanages brought in volunteers to comfort and hold the infants, and the infants immediately began to develop normally again.

If you are not valued, you will suffer negative consequences. If you grow up in an environment where you are not appreciated, or you perceive that you are not wanted, you will develop a low perception of value. This means that, at least on a subconscious level, you perceive yourself as not being important or valued to those around you. This perception stimulates the emotion of *worthlessness* – a feeling that you are alienated, isolated, alone and unwanted. If the emotion of worthlessness is strong enough, it will often times lead to depression.

Because being accepted by those around you is such a strong survival need, when you have the perception that you are not valued, you will behave in ways to try to achieve acceptance. This could be something as small as wanting to make sure your waiter sees you leaving a good tip, wanting to be acknowledged for giving the most expensive gift, or wanting people to see you in your expensive car. It may even lead to addictions to sex, compulsive spending, or overeating.

On the other hand, if you grow up in an environment where you are appreciated and respected, you develop the perception that you are valued. In turn, you experience the positive emotion of *joy*, rather than worthlessness, and the need to gain acknowledgement and acceptance from others is simply not there. People with a high perception of value will tend to be more expressive, communicative and creative. Because they tend to be more upbeat and happy than their low-value counterparts, they tend to attract many more friends and have a better support system during times of difficulty.

How much control do I have over myself and the world around me?

Your survival also depends on your ability to have some control over the world around you. When you feel in control, you feel *empowered*. You feel like you can handle anything that the world throws at you. On the other hand, if you feel as though you are unable to cope with even minor problems, or that you have no control over anything, you will quickly become very distressed and *anxious*. Whether you experience the emotions of empowerment or anxiety will depend again on your early childhood experiences.

If you grow up in an environment where you feel that you have a good deal of control over your life and are encouraged to be independent, you develop the subconscious perception of effectiveness; that you are in control of your environment. This perception of effectiveness stimulates the positive emotion of empowerment, and because of this emotion, you will be motivated to proactively create change in your world. Those with a high perception of effectiveness will tend to be more entrepreneurial, comfortable with risk, and will feel more comfortable relying on their talents and skills when faced with problem-solving, than their low-effectiveness counterparts.

On the other hand, if you grow up in an environment where you have little or no control over your life and where others constantly undermine you or find fault with what you do, you will develop the perception of ineffectiveness. If you have the perception that you have little or no control over your environment, you will experience the emotion of anxiety. Anxiety is one of the emotions that stimulates what is called the "fight, flight or freeze" response. This response is experienced as an urgent desire to retaliate, escape, or just freeze in a situation which you perceive as dangerous or threatening. You may experience anxiety as a sense of panic in social situations. You may often feel overwhelmed by financial or relationship pressures and feel a sense of desperation or even entertain thoughts of suicide.

How predictable or chaotic is my world?

Human beings are creatures who thrive on organization and structure. Organization and structure offers something very important for survival:

predictability. If the world is chaotic and unpredictable we will always have to be on guard for unforeseen dangers. This greatly interferes with our ability to form relationships and seek out new experiences, because all of our energy is spent in a constant need to defend ourselves. On the other hand, if the world is a predictable place, we do not have to worry that danger is lurking around every corner. We can let down our guard a bit and spend our energy developing relationships with other people.

Because predictability is important for your survival, one of the questions you had to answer for yourself when you first arrived in the world was whether your world was predictable or chaotic. If your early experiences are very consistent – regular feeding times, same caregivers, same home – you will develop the perception that the world is a structured and organized place. The emotion of *confidence* which arises from having this perception motivates you be curious, to seek out new experiences and to develop trust in those around you.

On the other hand, if you grow up in an environment where there the only thing constant is change, and there is much unpredictability and uncertainty in the expectations placed on you, the discipline your parents dole out, where you live, or even who is raising you, a very different perception of the world will develop. Instead of perceiving the world as a place which is predictable, you will perceive that the world is chaotic. This perception leads to experiencing the emotion of *stress*.

It is important to note that any perceived threat to the structure in your life results in the emotion of stress, no matter whether your perception is that the world is predictable or unpredictable. Stress can be caused by just about any change: losing a job, getting a new job, a death in the family, having a new baby, losing your home, buying a new home; whether the change is positive or negative does not matter. Stress will be experienced whenever there is a change in the structure of your life. Stress can become overwhelming, however, if you have the subconscious perception that the world is highly unpredictable. You may not be aware that you have this perception, only that you feel very stressed much of the time.

How hostile or nurturing is my world?

Throughout history, people have had to survive through wars, wild animal attacks, epidemics, natural disasters, famine, social unrest and crime. Consequently, those who had developed the ability to perceive these dangers early and avoid them were the ones who tended to survive and pass this 'danger-perceiving' attribute on to their children. It was a system of ensuring the survival of mankind. When a person experienced an event which they perceived as being a threat to their life or well-being, the emotion of *fear* took over, encouraging the person to take whatever action was necessary to stay alive. As you might expect, fear is the other emotion that stimulates the "fight, flight or freeze" response.

Now that was a great system way back in the early days of humankind's development, but the problem is that today, when our world is largely devoid of plagues, famine and other significant dangers, this system does not cease to exist. Rather, your subconscious perception of hostility continues to grope for signs of danger wherever it can; the whole point is to avoid peril. When few life-threatening dangers exist, your perception of hostility will shift its focus onto less significant, non-life-threatening "dangers" and you will begin to experience fearful emotions toward them as though they were, in-fact, significant and life-threatening. If you are fortunate enough to be so situated in life that most of your needs and desires are being met, you can actually begin to react negatively to perceived dangers which are completely fabricated in your subconscious.

The woman who became upset over the cheddar fondue in the

beginning of the Introduction was suffering from this phenomenon. Although the cheddar fondue was not a threat to her life, her subconscious seized upon that event as being symbolic of the world being a hostile place. Her behavior then was just the manifestation of the emotional response she experienced.

If you grow up in an environment which is nurturing and with the feeling that you are safe, you will develop the perception that the world is a nurturing place and not a threat to you. The emotion generated by the perception that the world is a nurturing place is called *attraction*; it motives us to interact with and engage other people, develop intimacy, care for other people and be emotionally available and supportive.

On the other hand, if you grow up in an environment that is very abusive or where you are frequently threatened, you will develop a perception that the world is hostile, which in turn will generate the emotion of fear. Those who experience constant fear are likely to become overly sensitive and defensive, may shun other people's company and can even develop social phobias.

Another important point about the perception that the world is a nurturing place: If you have this perception and you experience the emotion of attraction, you will find it much easier to maintain intimate relationships than do those who have the perception that the world is hostile and who experience fear. Attraction is the single-most important emotion within a marriage because the degree of intimacy you experience with your partner is in direct proportion to the degree you perceive that the relationship is nurturing.

Emotions and Feelings

Your feelings are divided into a set of non-emotions, such as feeling tired, feeling alert, feeling calm or feeling melancholy, as well as a set of feelings called emotions. Your primary emotions include: fear, anxiety, stress, worthlessness, joy, confidence, empowerment and attraction. This set of emotions differs from other types of non-emotional feelings in a number of important ways:

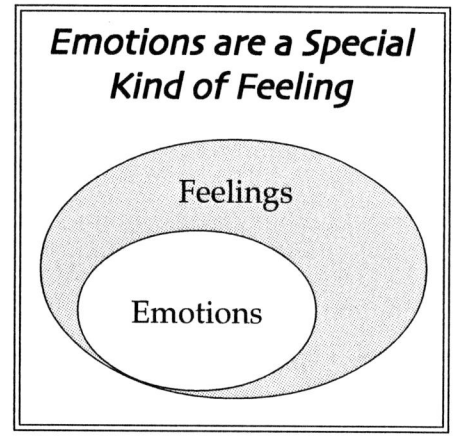

- Emotions happen quickly. If you are laid off from your job, you will experience stress the moment you receive your pink slip. But if you drive by a billboard advertising a mattress, you won't instantly become tired. Non-emotional feelings have a much more gradual onset - they don't have a distinct starting point like emotions do.
- Emotions are designed to be an important *external* survival mechanism, and to help you cope with the external environment. Non-emotional feelings are designed to help you maintain your *internal* balance, and to help satisfy your body's needs. If you feel tired, you will want to sleep; if you feel hungry, you will want to eat. Emotions will motivate you to interact with the world around you to avoid dangers and form relationships, but non-emotional feelings will not.
- Emotions carry with them a sense of urgency, but non-emotion feelings do not. You have probably experienced how emotions fill you with a sense of urgency. When you feel fear, for example, there is an immediate

readiness to defend yourself or to escape as quickly as possible. When you experience the emotion of attraction when you meet someone you are interested in, you experience a sense of urgency; the urgency to be with them, to talk to them, that person is all you can think about. This sense of urgency is not found in non-emotional feelings.

The important idea here is that while all emotions are feelings, not all feelings are emotions. You have two types of feelings, emotional feelings and non-emotional feelings. Both are designed to help you survive, but while your non-emotional feelings help you take care of your internal needs, your emotions help you cope with the challenges of the external world.

You Respond Emotionally to Meaningful Events

Whenever you respond to an event in an emotional way, it is because your subconscious perceptions see something in the event that is meaningful to you; it supports one of your four perceptions about yourself or your world. For example, if you receive a gift from someone, or someone holds the door open for you, you will have a positive emotional response because you perceive that you are valued. But if someone threatens you, you will have a negative emotional response because you perceive hostility. The fact is that *every time you respond emotionally to an event it is because you perceive that the event has some meaning about you and your environment.*

As will be discussed later in this chapter, your perceptions are what assign meaning to the events in your life. What this means is that how you perceive your self and your world will dictate what emotions you experience. An important point to note is that your perceptions will influence your emotional response to just about every event. For example, when you have the perception that you are not valued, you will tend to interpret every event as evidence that you are not valued. I call this phenomenon the *perceptive filter*.

Your Perceptive Filter

Your perceptive filter is responsible for influencing or dictating your emotional response to a particular event. This can be positive or negative, depending on whether your perceptions are positive or negative. If your perceptions are positive, you will tend to filter out those events which are negative, and will subconsciously focus only on those events which trigger positive emotional responses. Conversely, if your perceptions are negative, you will filter out those events which are positive, and will subconsciously focus only on those events which trigger negative emotional responses.

Here's how that works. As we will discuss a little bit later, your subconscious does not handle factual information, but rather symbolic or emotional information. Your subconscious is not concerned with the specifics surrounding an event, just what the event means to you emotionally. Consequently, the facts about any situation – whether you are in the corporate board room or in your private bedroom, whether you are having a conflict with your spouse or your boss – are ignored by the subconscious. But remember, your perceptions lie in your subconscious, and these are what generate specific emotions. So your perceptions act as a guide of sorts; if you respond to the event with a particular emotion, and that emotion conforms with other emotions generated by your perceptions, that emotion is perceived as "valid," or "meaningful." If the emotional meaning of the event as perceived by the subconscious is not in accordance with your perception, that event will be rather meaningless to you.

For example, say you have a low perception of value. If you appeal to your boss for a raise and are denied, you will believe that you were denied the raise because you are not valued by your boss. Because this belief accords with your low perception of value, this event will have significant emotional meaning for you. On the other hand, if you have a high perception of value, and you appeal to your boss for a raise and are denied, you will have no reason to believe that you are not valued by your boss; you will likely prescribe some other reason for the denial of the raise, and the event will have little meaning to you emotionally.

The stronger your perceptions are, the more pronounced your perceptive filter is, and the more intensely you will feel the emotions produced by your perceptions.

Here's an illustration of that point, again using the perception of value. Depression is the condition which results from the intense, recurrent emotion of worthlessness. The emotion of worthlessness is created by a low perception of value. When you are depressed, you will tend to perceive all events as evidence that you are not a good person; that you are not valued. Because of this, you will react with the same emotion of worthlessness regardless of whether someone fails to call you back, forgets to give you an expected gift or cuts you off in traffic. Because you are depressed, however, you will react much more strongly to these situations than would someone who doesn't have quite as low perception of value as you do; you feel the emotional response to these events - worthlessness - in extreme measure.

Even if something good happens, like someone tries to befriend you, your perceptive filter will take over and either negate the event entirely, or turn it from being a positive event to a being negative event in some way. Instead of feeling excited that someone wants to be your friend, your perceptive filter may generate the feeling of worthlessness, and make you think that this other person only likes you because they don't know you very well; if this person were to get to know you and see who you really are, they wouldn't like you anymore.

Your perceptive filter, because it is made up of your own unique blend of perceptions, will differ from other people's. You may be in a group of people who experience the same event, yet you will all walk away with a very different emotional experience based on your emotional filter. Let's take the event of getting some constructive criticism as an example. If you suffer from a perception that the world is hostile, and you experience fear, you may see constructive criticism or suggestions from others as evidence that you are being attacked. If you have a low perception of value and experience worthlessness, you may see constructive criticism or suggestions from others as evidence that you are somehow not a good person. If you suffer from a low perception of effectiveness, and you experience anxiety, you may see constructive criticism as evidence that you are ineffective. If you have a perception that the world is chaotic and you suffer from stress, you may see constructive criticism as evidence that there is a crisis and everything needs to change.

When I worked in sales, the company I worked for was experiencing a slump in sales. The management was looking for ideas on how to improve our sales during the slow time, so they held a meeting with all of the sales people and opened the floor up for ideas. After about a half an hour of brainstorming, our manager began to wrap up the meeting. He concluded by encouraging us to spend extra time and effort with each client and if we needed help closing a deal to get one of the sales managers or a more experienced sales person involved. He wished us luck, and said that he felt confident that we would be able to meet the corporate sales projection if we just make the extra effort for each client. The meeting adjourned and we all went back to our offices. I thought the meeting was fairly calm and cordial, as far as sales meetings go.

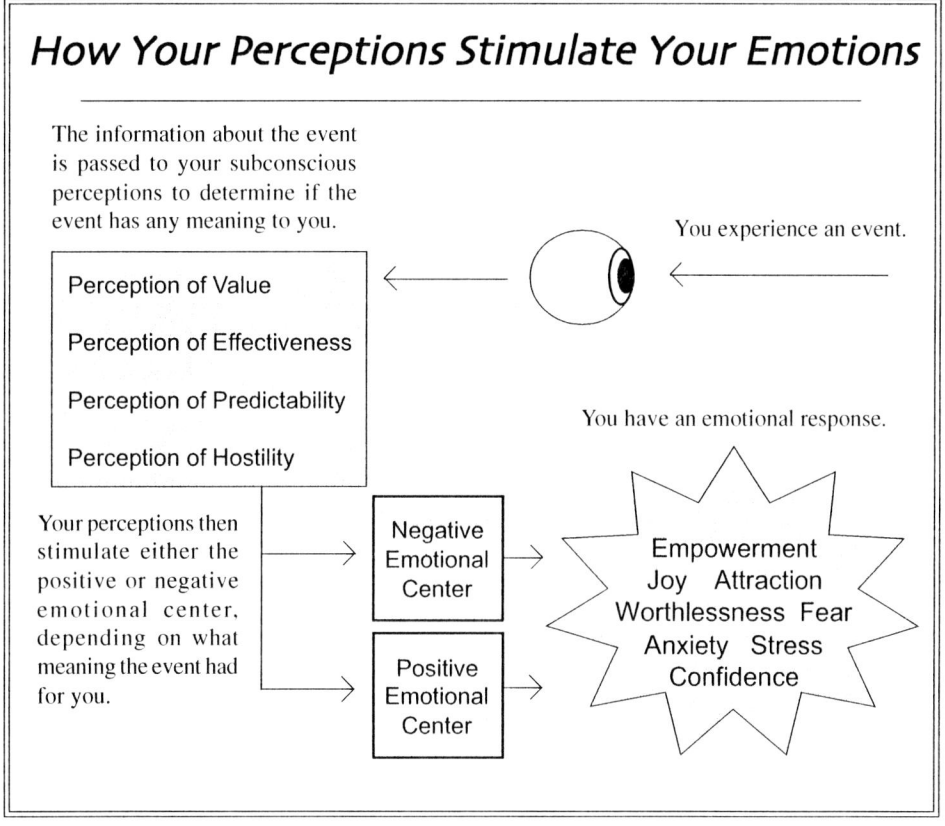

About ten minutes after the meeting another sales person came to my office and asked me if I had a moment to talk. I nodded and she sat down. She started the conversation by asking, "can you believe the way they treated us up there?" I had no idea what she was referring to, so I asked, "what do you mean?" She replied, "can you believe the way they freaked out on us in that meeting? The sales manager just screamed at us." I told her that we must have been in different meetings because that was not the experience I had at all. There was no time that anyone pointed fingers, raised their voice, spoke in a disrespectful way, or anything of the kind.

Although my co-worker and I had been sitting side-by-side in the same room, we experienced two very different meetings. She experienced a meeting that was hostile, where I experienced a meeting that was cordial. The difference in our experience was all in how we perceived the events at the meeting. Based on our perceptions, our perceptive filter dictated our emotional responses, which in turn influenced our individual experiences. We were at the same meeting, but it had a very different emotional meaning for each of us.

Now that we have spent some time discussing how our perceptions look for meaning in the events in our life, and how this meaning is what is responsible for creating the emotional responses we experience, let's take a look at how your emotions are generated in your brain, and discuss each of your eight primary emotions.

Your Two Emotional Centers

There are two distinct emotional centers in your brain which are responsible for creating the emotions you experience every day. One emotional center is responsible for generating positive emotions, and one emotional center is responsible for generating negative emotions. Both of these centers are located in a single specialized structure in the brain called the *amygdala*. The amygdala is part of a group of structures in the brain called the limbic system, and is the main structure involved with all aspects of emotion from generating the emotions themselves, to recognizing emotional facial expressions.

When you experience an emotion, it is because one or the other, or both, of these emotional centers in the amygdala have been stimulated. If the positive emotional center is stimulated, you will experience one of the positive emotions of confidence, joy, attraction or empowerment. The positive emotional center, also called the *appetitive center*, is designed to aid your survival by driving you to form relationships with other people and to seek out novel experiences. Positive emotions are *proactive*. This means you will seek out ways to express the emotion. The positive emotions of joy, empowerment, attraction and confidence are experienced when you feel personally valued and effective, and you live in a social structure which is nurturing and stable. In the absence of perceived threats, your positive emotional center is more active. This means that if you can reduce your negative emotions, positive emotions will emerge all by themselves. Taking away negative emotions is like removing a plastic covering from the top of a garden. Just by removing the cover which was keeping anything from growing, your garden will soon be filled with beauty and life.

If the negative emotional center is stimulated, you experience one of the negative emotions of fear, stress, anxiety or worthlessness. The negative emotional center, also called the *aversive center*, is designed to aid your survival by driving you to avoid situations which are hazardous to you. An important point to remember about negative emotions; they are *reactive emotions*, which means that you will only express those emotions by reacting to events in your environment. The negative emotions of depression, anxiety, stress and fear are experienced when you feel that you are not valued and are ineffective in controlling your environment, and you live in a social structure which is hostile and chaotic. Because negative emotions are intended to keep you out of danger, they will be more intense than positive emotions. Your mind figures it's better to be safe than to be happy.

Your Four Perceptions and Eight Primary Emotions

In this section you will learn about your eight primary emotions and how they are created by your four perceptions of value, effectiveness, predictability and hostility. Each perception is responsible for generating two emotions – one positive and one negative.

Your Perception of Value Creates the Emotions of Joy and Worthlessness

Joy is the positive emotion experienced when you have the perception of being valued, and can be described as a feeling of contentment, happiness and that your life has meaning. One of the things that sets human beings apart from other animals is our need to find meaning in life; we need to feel as though our life has some value. The psychologist Viktor Frankl, who wrote *Man's Search for Meaning* after surviving three years in Nazi death camps, developed a type of therapy he called *logotherapy*. The whole point of logotherapy was to identify the meaning in the individual's life and to work to develop a strong connection to that meaning. "Why don't you just commit suicide?" Viktor would ask his clients. The answer that his client gave indicated what meaning they saw in their life. Although Viktor didn't

---

Depression and the Emotion of Worthlessness

Far too many people go through life feeling dissatisfied and depressed, but they don't know why. The National Institutes of Mental Health estimates that one out of every ten adults in the United States suffers from depression every year; a 300% increase over the past ten years. It is estimated that by the year 2020, depression will be the number one cause of disability in the United States.

Since depression is caused by the emotion of worthlessness, it is more important than ever for us all to learn how to understand and master our emotional state.

identify it this way, what he was really asking people was what value they perceived in themselves. Those who perceive a lot of value experience a great deal of joy and happiness. Those who perceive that they have little value experience the opposite. They will tend to experience the emotion of worthlessness.

Worthlessness is the negative emotion experienced when you have the perception of not being valued; that your life has no meaning. If you suffer from depression, what you are really suffering from is a chronic emotion of worthlessness created by a low perception of value. This low perception of value may make you feel as though unfortunate events, in which you played no part, are somehow your fault; that any negative event in your life just reinforces your conviction that *everything* in your life is bad; that experiences which would indicate that you are valued and loved, somehow don't really count; that nobody would like you once they really got to know you, or in some cases, that it really didn't matter if you lived or died.

Your Perception of Effectiveness Creates the Emotions of Empowerment and Anxiety

Empowerment is the positive emotion experienced when you have the perception that you can successfully control what happens in your life. The business world is full of programs designed to help people develop this emotion. All of the big names like Zig Ziglar, Tony Robbins and Hyrum Smith have spent their life with one goal in mind: to get people to understand that they have the power to control the events in their life; that they make their own destiny. These programs are so popular because it has been proven time and time again that when people feel in control of their life, they are more productive, happier and healthier. They feel this way because they experience the emotion of empowerment.

If you had a time in your life where you felt like everything was under control, like you could handle anything that came your way, like you were the master of your own destiny, then you know what this emotion feels like. You may have felt the opposite as well – if you have had a time in your life when you felt as if everything was out of control; as if your problems were insurmountable – you have experienced anxiety.

Anxiety is the negative emotion experienced when you have the perception that you have no control over the events in your environment. Anxiety can be described as kind of a panicky-sick feeling associated with feeling out of control or unable to cope. If you are addicted to shopping, drinking or gambling, you will typically experience the feeling of bewilderment and frustration over your actions. You may avoid certain social situations or intimate relationships, because of a feeling of being overwhelmed. When you experience anxiety it is because at the subconscious level, you feel that you are not able to handle situations which confront you very effectively.

There was an interesting study that was done many years ago involving rats. In this experiment, the rats were in a cage with a wire floor divided down the middle by a short wall. The researchers flashed a light in the cage, followed quickly by an electric shock to the floor of the cage on the side where the rat was sitting. The first time this happened, the rat felt confused and became pretty upset. But the rat discovered that he could escape the shock by jumping over the short wall to the other side of the cage whenever he saw the light flash. Soon, every time the researchers flashed the light, the rat jumped over the short wall and avoided the shock altogether. The rat had figured out what actions he needed to take in order to avoid pain. As long as the rat could take this action to avoid the shock, he showed no signs of anxiety or distress.

At one point the researchers changed the experiment so that the rat could no longer escape from the shock when the light flashed. To everyone's surprise, after a very short time, when the rat discovered that he no longer had control over whether he would experience the shock or not, the rat just sat there and wouldn't move; he just accepted the pain of the electric shock. The rat became apathetic and showed signs of being distressed.

Although this experiment was with a rat, the same thing happens with you. If you feel as though no matter what you do, you cannot avoid pain, you cannot exercise control over the events in your life, or if you feel that forces are at work in your life which you do not understand, you will suffer from the emotion of anxiety.

Your Perception of Predictability Creates the Emotions of Confidence and Stress

People are creatures who thrive on structure. We form habits and create routine for ourselves. Even the community in which we live is run by a very extensive and complicated system of rules and standards of behavior for us all to follow called law. When someone breaks the law, the victim and the community experience stress and the law-breaker is punished. This need for predictability and structure is found in other aspects of society also, and can be so intense that even thoughts and ideas can create enough stress for the society to punish or rebel against an individual or a group who represents a non-conforming viewpoint. At times, this need for conformity will make us act in ways contrary to our nature, or even to contradict what we know to be the truth.

In the 1950s a researcher named S.E. Asche conducted a series of studies where six individuals were shown a line of a certain length and told to choose one of three other lines of varying lengths that matched it. Prior to the experiment, five of the six individuals were secretly instructed to choose one of the incorrect answers. The sixth person was completely unaware that the other five had been instructed to pick a specific line. The naïve subject was placed so that they could hear the answers of the other five subjects before they made their own decision. Asche concluded that "under this form of social pressure, a large fraction of subjects went along with the group rather than accept the unmistakable evidence of their own eyes."

We try to create as much uniformity, structure and organization as possible because it helps us feel secure in a world that offers many threats to our security - where natural disasters and plagues threaten our survival with random death and destruction. We recognize that we need other people to help us survive, and so we attempt to conform with society's standards and find a place of belonging within that society. When we feel that society is not arbitrarily created – that everyone lives by the same set of rules – then we feel much more confident about our place within that society.

When you perceive that your life and the world around you is organized, structured and predictable, you will feel calm and free of worry. This is the emotion of confidence. Confidence is experienced when you perceive that the world is predictable; that you can know beforehand what is going to happen and how you will act. On the other hand, when your life's structure or organization changes, you no longer have the ability to be confident about what is going to happen. Consequently, you experience the opposite emotion of stress.

As illustrated before, stress occurs whenever your life changes in some way. If you have a new member of the family, a new job, or you are going out on a blind date, you experience stress because you find yourself in a situation where things are unpredictable. You can experience stress even by *anticipating* that something may change, as when your employer is laying off workers and you don't know whether you will lose your job.

Stress Associated With Life-Changing Events

Excerpt from:
Holmes T., Masuda M. (1972) Psychosomatic Syndrome. *Psychology Today*, April, 71

Rank	Life Event	Life Change Units
1	death of spouse	100
2	divorce	73
3	marital separation	65
4	jail term	63
5	death of a close family member	63
6	personal injury or illness	53
7	marriage	50
8	fired at work	47
9	marital reconciliation	45
10	retirement	45
11	change in health of a family member	44
12	pregnancy	40
13	sex difficulties	39
14	gain of new family member	39
15	change in financial state	38
16	change to different line of work	36
17	mortgage or loan for major purchase	31
18	foreclosure of mortgage or loan	30
19	change in responsibilities at work	29
20	child leaving home	29
21	trouble with in-laws	29
22	outstanding personal achievement	28
23	spouse begins or stops work	26
24	change in living conditions	25
25	trouble with your boss	23
26	change in work hours	20
27	change in residence	20
28	change in school	20
29	change in social activities	18
30	minor violation of the law	11

Scoring: 0 – 150:   No Significant Problems
         150 – 199:   Mild Life Crisis
         200 – 299:   Moderate Life Crisis
         300 or more: Major Life Crisis

If you grew up in a home where you never knew what was expected of you, where you moved a lot, or there was no constancy in who was raising you, you will have developed the perception that the world is very unpredictable. Because humans are so driven for predictability and structure, this perception will cause you to experience a lot of stress.

Your Perception of Hostility Creates the Emotions of Attraction and Fear

Attraction is the positive emotion experienced when you have the perception that your environment is a kind and nurturing place. The emotion of attraction is kind of like the feeling of belonging, or the feeling of connectedness and intimacy. When you experience this emotion you seek out to develop relationships, become active in your community, and give of yourself. Intimacy in a marriage is entirely dependant on the emotion of attraction.

The positive emotion of attraction motivates you to bond with other people. This emotion is so strong that if you feel alienated from other people, you will feel very frightened. Many people will remain in relationships, religious groups or community organizations, even if they are treated poorly, just so that they can avoid the feeling of isolation. The social psychologist Erich Fromm echoed this truth about people in his book *Escape From Freedom* when he said:

"Religion and nationalism, as well as any custom and any belief however absurd and degrading, if it only connects the individual with others, are refuges from what man most dreads: isolation."

Fear is the negative emotion experienced when you have the

perception that your environment is a hostile and dangerous place. Fear is the most powerful of all emotions and will elicit the strongest negative emotional response. If you have ever been attacked by a dog, had someone try to break into your house or been followed when you were walking alone, you have experienced the emotion of fear. Even if you have never lived through these frightening events, I'm sure you have experienced the emotion of fear. Most of the time fear is experienced as the feeling that people are threatening you in some way by what they say or do.

The negative emotion of fear takes a different approach to help us meet our need for security by motivating us to avoid the danger altogether, or if that is not possible, to prepare us physiologically for a fight. Whereas the positive emotion of attraction helps us fulfill our need for security through bonding with other people, the negative emotion of fear helps us fulfill our need for security through avoidance, withdrawal or aggression.

There are many situations where we might experience both of these emotions at the same time. For example, on September 11, 2001, when the World Trade Center was attacked by foreign terrorists, the country experienced tremendous fear, as demonstrated by the huge increase in the sales of home security devices, guns, gas masks and personal security services, as well as a tremendous increase in the demand for mental health counseling services.

But people also experienced attraction. Families who hadn't spent much time with one another suddenly felt drawn closer together, and individuals who hadn't been active in their churches, synagogues, mosques or covens suddenly felt compelled to bond with others in their religious communities. There was also a huge swell of patriotism as people sought to bond with their fellow citizens. I was one of the many people in my town who purchased a large flag and hung it on the side of my house. The feeling was that everyone needed to stick together to fight off this new threat.

An interesting phenomenon about attraction and fear, is that as long as the threat and fear come from a source outside of our relationships with other people, like in the example of the World Trade Center attack, the emotion of attraction will motivate us to form closer relationships. However, if the threat and fear come from within a relationship, the emotion of fear will overpower the emotion of attraction and those within the relationship will not draw closer, but pull further apart.

I'm sure you know married couples who have expressed a frustration that their relationship has lost its intimacy, and they no longer feel as close as they used to feel. Tracing back through their history, you invariably find that the disintegration of their intimacy began when they started arguing or fighting. Fights, whether verbal or physical, are perceived as threats to security. Each time you fight with someone, you develop a stronger and stronger perception of hostility – a threat associated with that other person. This perception, this threat, stimulates the emotion of fear, and fear motivates you to withdraw from the situation. Since you cannot experience the emotion of attraction and fear toward the same person, and since the negative emotion of fear is more powerful, fear will create a breakdown of intimacy.

Secondary Emotions

Secondary emotions are also called interpreted emotions because they require processing from the conscious mind in order to be elicited. For example, if you are driving in your car and someone runs a red light and nearly hits you, the immediate primary emotions you feel may be fear and stress. You experience fear because you perceive that the car which ran the red light poses a very real threat to you. You experience stress because of the unpredictable nature of the event.

After a few moments, those emotions of fear and stress combine forces and turn into the secondary emotion of anger. Angry thoughts enter your head, such as, "they could have killed me because they weren't paying attention!" Or, "how can people keep their license when they drive so recklessly?!" The emotion of anger only arises *after* you have an initial emotional response *and* your conscious mind passes judgement on the appropriateness of the actions of others.

Your conscious judgements of how other people act or how the world works are called emotionally-linked expectations. These emotionally-linked expectations create the secondary emotional response. So, in the example above, the anger you experienced only occurred after your conscious mind judged the other person's behavior to be inappropriate.

There is little doubt that as you go through your day you are exposed to the actions of others that you judge as being inappropriate or "bad." So why don't you respond to all of these actions? Because *you will only experience a secondary emotion if you first experience a primary emotion.* You may not like someone else's behavior, but if you don't subconsciously perceive that their behavior means anything to you emotionally, you will not have a primary emotional response. Consequently, you will not have a secondary emotional response either.

This means that *if you are experiencing any of the secondary emotions, such as anger, desperation, withdrawal, apathy, disappointment or guarding, it is because you are experiencing fear, anxiety, stress or worthlessness first*. In order to overcome difficulties with the secondary emotions, you have to address the primary emotions.

Listed below are six common secondary emotions which most people experience at one time or another. While this discussion may leave the impression that the secondary emotions are only negative, this is not the case. There are plenty of positive secondary emotions; hope, love, anticipation and excitement are just a few. I want to focus here on the negative secondary emotions, however, because these are the secondary emotions which cause the most problems for most people.

Anger

Anger arises out of a combination of the two primary emotions of fear and worthlessness. When you become angry, it is typically because you perceive that someone has acted in a way that is a threat to you or is disrespectful.

Desperation

Desperation arises out of a combination of the two primary emotions of worthlessness and anxiety. When you feel desperate, it is typically because you feel that your life is hopelessly out of control, usually coupled with the feeling of worthlessness.

Rage and Withdrawal

Rage and withdrawal arise out of a combination of the two most potent negative emotions: anxiety and fear. Each of these emotions will stimulate the "fight, flight or freeze" response. When taken together, they have an even more powerful effect. An example of this secondary emotion occurs if you get robbed on the street. You will experience fear in that situation, because the threat to your safety is real. Unless you are a trained fighter, you will also experience anxiety – the feeling of being out of control of the situation.

Apathy

Apathy arises out of a combination of the emotions of stress and anxiety. When you experience apathy, you feel as though there is no way of knowing what the future holds, and even if there were, you feel as though you would be powerless to change it.

Disappointment

Disappointment arises out of a combination of the emotions of stress and worthlessness. A situation where this secondary emotion can arise is one which most people have experienced, such as when you hold a party and most of the people you've invited don't show up. When this happens, the unpredictability of the event creates the emotion of stress. Also, the emotion of worthlessness is stimulated because your subconscious sees the event as evidence that other people – the invitees – don't value you.

Guarding

Guarding arises out of a combination of the emotions of stress and fear and creates an "us versus them" feeling. For example, prior to the attacks of September 11, 2001, it seemed that nobody in the United States could get along. The in-fighting among special interest, minority and political groups was heated and pervasive. Once the attacks occurred, however, there was a resurgence of patriotism unlike anything seen since the Second World War. Instead of the New York Police force being the villains, they suddenly became the heroes. This sudden change in public sentiment occurred because we felt the stress of the unpredictability of the event, coupled with the fear of the danger the attacks represented.

Developing Emotional Awareness

A big challenge for those who want to improve their emotional state is developing an awareness of what emotions they are feeling. Because emotions are so often seen as the unimportant touchy-feely stuff and are not taken very seriously – even by many psychologists – most people have lost much of their awareness of what emotions they are experiencing. I can't tell you how many times I had felt depressed or angry or just generally restless and irritable and people asked me what was wrong, and I was unable to tell them. I just didn't know. There were a lot of things I could point to such as bad traffic or that my girlfriend didn't call me when she said she would, but these were not the real cause of the problem. Most of the time, I did not know whether I felt stressed, or fearful or anxious. I just knew that I felt very unhappy.

My experience is not unique. I have worked with a lot of people over the years to help them improve their lives and, invariably, the first obstacle that they needed to overcome was their inability to identify what emotions they were experiencing. They needed to develop some degree of emotional awareness.

The reason that this is so important is that our emotions can help us decipher our subconscious perceptions. Because our perceptions reside in the subconscious, we cannot be aware of them directly. We can only see what emotions they produce in different circumstances. As a matter of fact, paying attention to how we react emotionally is the *only* way we can figure out the condition of our perceptions, and if we cannot identify what emotions we are experiencing, we will be flying blind in our effort to change our perceptions.

To Sum Up About Your Perceptions and Emotions

In this chapter you learned that emotions are one type of feeling you experience, and that there are a number of other feelings you can experience, such as feeling tired, that are not emotions. You learned that emotions are generated whenever you experience something which you perceive as being meaningful to you, and that the collection of your perceptions create an perceptive filter. Your perceptive filter will tend to generate a recurrent pattern of emotions regardless of what events occur – you will tend to emotionally respond in very predictable ways to all situations, no matter how factually different from one another they might be. You learned about each of your eight primary emotions and how they are created by your four perceptions, and how your primary emotions can form secondary emotions. Finally, you learned about the importance of being able to identify what emotion you are experiencing so that you can work to change the underlying perception, if the emotion is making you unhappy.

One idea that is important to understand is that you can't always believe what you think or what you feel. Because of the phenomenon of your perceptive filter, you will subconsciously look for evidence to support your perceptions, and disregard experiences which would support an alternative perception. Consequently, you will be convinced that your thoughts and emotions reflect reality, when in fact they don't. When you are experiencing negative emotions, I urge you to keep in mind that in all likelihood, half of what you believe and feel is probably wrong – you just don't know which half. So don't take what you feel too seriously.

Exercise

Developing Emotional Awareness

~~~~~~~~~~~~~~~~~~~~~~~~~~~~

The purpose of this exercise is to help you develop an awareness of how you feel. This is important because you can't change what you feel until you know what you feel. Over the next three days, write down what is going on around you and what emotions you are experiencing as you go through your day. On the fourth day, you will look back over the previous three days to look for patterns in the emotions you experienced.

It takes some practice to develop emotional awareness, so don't worry if are not sure what emotion you are experiencing. Just take your best guess and do the exercise to the best of your ability. You may not feel that your life has been transformed by this exercise. That is okay. The intent is to make you more aware of what emotions you experience so you can identify what you want to change. An example is on the next page.

Developing Emotional Awareness - Example

Time | Current Situation

9:00 am When I arrived at work, I found out that I had to give a presentation at 10:00.

Secondary Emotion: _Angry - because they didn't tell me earlier_

Primary Emotion: ☒ Fear ☒ Stress ☒ Anxiety ☐ Worthlessness
☐ Attraction ☐ Confidence ☐ Empowerment ☐ Joy

1:00 pm The presentation went well, but because I had to do it, I had to work through lunch to get the rest of my stuff done.

Secondary Emotion: _Frustrated and stressed out_

Primary Emotion: ☐ Fear ☒ Stress ☐ Anxiety ☐ Worthlessness
☐ Attraction ☐ Confidence ☐ Empowerment ☐ Joy

6:00 pm Got home a bit early because the traffic was good. Ordering a pizza for dinner.

Secondary Emotion: _Calm, but a bit burned out from the day_

Primary Emotion: ☐ Fear ☒ Stress *a little* ☐ Anxiety ☐ Worthlessness
☐ Attraction ☐ Confidence ☐ Empowerment ☒ Joy?

9:00 pm Listening to the news - another company is claiming bankruptcy.

Secondary Emotion: _Angry at the politicians who let this happen_

Primary Emotion: ☒ Fear? ☒ Stress ☐ Anxiety ☐ Worthlessness
☐ Attraction ☐ Confidence ☐ Empowerment ☐ Joy

Developing Emotional Awareness - Day 1

Time   Current Situation

9:00 am   _____

              Secondary Emotion: _____

              Primary Emotion: ☐ Fear   ☐ Stress   ☐ Anxiety   ☐ Worthlessness
                                   ☐ Attraction   ☐ Confidence   ☐ Empowerment   ☐ Joy

1:00 pm   _____

              Secondary Emotion: _____

              Primary Emotion: ☐ Fear   ☐ Stress   ☐ Anxiety   ☐ Worthlessness
                                   ☐ Attraction   ☐ Confidence   ☐ Empowerment   ☐ Joy

6:00 pm   _____

              Secondary Emotion: _____

              Primary Emotion: ☐ Fear   ☐ Stress   ☐ Anxiety   ☐ Worthlessness
                                   ☐ Attraction   ☐ Confidence   ☐ Empowerment   ☐ Joy

9:00 pm   _____

              Secondary Emotion: _____

              Primary Emotion: ☐ Fear   ☐ Stress   ☐ Anxiety   ☐ Worthlessness
                                   ☐ Attraction   ☐ Confidence   ☐ Empowerment   ☐ Joy

Developing Emotional Awareness - Day 2

| Time | Current Situation |

9:00 am _____

Secondary Emotion: _____

Primary Emotion: ☐ Fear ☐ Stress ☐ Anxiety ☐ Worthlessness
☐ Attraction ☐ Confidence ☐ Empowerment ☐ Joy

1:00 pm _____

Secondary Emotion: _____

Primary Emotion: ☐ Fear ☐ Stress ☐ Anxiety ☐ Worthlessness
☐ Attraction ☐ Confidence ☐ Empowerment ☐ Joy

6:00 pm _____

Secondary Emotion: _____

Primary Emotion: ☐ Fear ☐ Stress ☐ Anxiety ☐ Worthlessness
☐ Attraction ☐ Confidence ☐ Empowerment ☐ Joy

9:00 pm _____

Secondary Emotion: _____

Primary Emotion: ☐ Fear ☐ Stress ☐ Anxiety ☐ Worthlessness
☐ Attraction ☐ Confidence ☐ Empowerment ☐ Joy

Developing Emotional Awareness - Day 3

Time	Current Situation

9:00 am _____

Secondary Emotion: _____

Primary Emotion: ☐ Fear ☐ Stress ☐ Anxiety ☐ Worthlessness
☐ Attraction ☐ Confidence ☐ Empowerment ☐ Joy

1:00 pm _____

Secondary Emotion: _____

Primary Emotion: ☐ Fear ☐ Stress ☐ Anxiety ☐ Worthlessness
☐ Attraction ☐ Confidence ☐ Empowerment ☐ Joy

6:00 pm _____

Secondary Emotion: _____

Primary Emotion: ☐ Fear ☐ Stress ☐ Anxiety ☐ Worthlessness
☐ Attraction ☐ Confidence ☐ Empowerment ☐ Joy

9:00 pm _____

Secondary Emotion: _____

Primary Emotion: ☐ Fear ☐ Stress ☐ Anxiety ☐ Worthlessness
☐ Attraction ☐ Confidence ☐ Empowerment ☐ Joy

Developing Emotional Awareness - Day 4

Over the past three days you have written down the emotions you experienced throughout the day. Take a look back over what you have written down and in the space below, give your interpretation of what you see. What emotions did you experience the most? Did you have a hard time identifying what primary emotion you were experiencing? Were there certain situations which seemed to make you react more than others?

_____

_____

_____

_____

_____

_____

_____

_____

_____

Chapter 2

Sensitivity and Emotional Intensity

~~~~~~~~~~~~~~~

"My life had been a series of beginnings without endings, projects started and never finished. Looking back I realized I had left unfinished many more tasks than I had ever finished. Somewhere out there in the 'unfinished task boneyard' lay hundreds of pieces of model airplanes and erector sets, wood intended for a fort, incomplete assignments, articles half-read, letters half-written, conversations half-listened to, and wonderful book titles and ideas conjured up but never used.

"It was fatiguing to think of all the opportunities I had passed up over the years because I could not focus on the steps of learning – thousands of ideas never followed through, wonderful ideas that were never given any dimension because they could not be taken far enough....

> *"The problem that dominated my life and shaped my personality was the need to avoid the piercing, rasping, blasting, disorganized chaos of incoming stimuli that I could not filter out, could not ignore. This made it hard for me to relate to other people; to think, study, and make it in school; to carry out tasks, plan ahead, remember. It embarrassed me and made me feel ashamed when I was with people; it made me insecure when I was alone....*
>
> *"My sensitivity to all stimuli increased as I grew older. Indoors or out, the space around me seemed flooded with sounds that were too loud, lights and colors that were too bright, odors that were too intense, tastes that were too strong, touches that were too harsh. I could not shut them out....*
>
> *Sensitivity to my environment was both a blessing and a curse. On the one hand, caring and empathy grew out of my heightened awareness of others. But on the other hand, when the volume went up, all I could think of was self-preservation. With every part of me I wanted to push the mess of my world aside and run...."*

(Excerpt from *Overload: Attention Deficit Disorder and the Addictive Brain* by David Miller)

In the excerpt above, David describes his experience with an aspect of the mind which is important to understand – *sensitivity*. Sensitivity refers to the intensity with which you experience information coming in from your five senses – sight, smell, hearing, touch and taste. If you have a high-sensitivity mind, you will experiences all of your senses much more intensely than someone with a low-sensitivity mind. Colors will be brighter, sounds will be louder, odors will be stronger, touch will feel more intense, and tastes will be stronger. As it turns out, how intensely you experience your emotions is also controlled by how intensely you experience your other senses. So if you have a high-sensitivity mind, you will experience all emotions intensely – good or bad.

In this chapter, you will learn how to identify and understand your own unique sensitivity and emotional intensity. You will learn how this level of emotional intensity affects your mood and your emotional volatility, and if you are a high-sensitivity person, how this will make you susceptible to experiencing emotional hijackings. Let's start out by learning where sensitivity comes from.

Introducing Sensitivity

You have a set of structures in your brain which are responsible for controlling how aware you are of your senses. I refer to this set of structures as your *sensory filter*. Your sensory filter has the job of filtering out information that is not important. For example, until I mentioned it, you were probably not aware of the feeling of the ground beneath your feet or the sensation of your shirt against your back. This is because your sensory filter deemed that information as not important and filtered it out instead of allowing it to clutter up your mind.

On the other hand, if you were walking and had a rock in your shoe, then you would be very aware of the feeling of the ground beneath your feet; especially that rock. This would be because the sensory filter decided that the rock in your shoe was important for you to be aware of since it could injure your foot. Once you remove the rock from your shoe, in a very short time you would again be unaware of how the ground felt under your feet.

Each person is a little bit different when it comes to how well this sensory filter works. If you filter out a lot of sensory information, you will not feel things through your senses very intensely than if you let more information in. When your sensory filter stops more than an average amount of sensation from reaching your awareness you have what's called a *low-*

sensitivity temperament. When you have a low-sensitivity temperament, you will require extra sensory information in order to experience the same sensation as an average person.

On the other end of the spectrum are those who don't filter out enough sensory information. If you don't filter out enough sensory information, your senses will be much more sensitive. When you experience more sensory information than the average person, you have what's called a *high-sensitivity temperament*. When you have a high-sensitivity temperament, you will become much more easily overwhelmed by sensory information and emotional intensity than the average person and will require very little sensory information to experience the same amount of sensation as the average person.

Your Sensitivity is Genetic, But...

When you are born, you come genetically programmed with a certain degree of sensitivity. Your sensory filter may shift somewhat toward a high-sensitivity depending on your experiences in the first few years of your life. After about four or five years of age, your sensory filter becomes permanently set in your mind. Once your sensory filter becomes fixed, it will not change to any appreciable degree throughout the rest of your lifetime. If you have a high-sensitivity temperament in childhood, you will also have a high-sensitivity temperament in adulthood.

The types of experiences which seem to have the greatest impact on the sensory filter during early childhood are traumatic events, such as abuse or neglect. Children who have been abused or neglected will experience a permanent shift toward a high-sensitivity temperament. This means that they will be permanently more emotionally volatile and sensitive than if they had not had those early traumatic experiences. The impact on emotional volatility of this upward shift becomes greater the higher the child's sensory filter was originally set by genetics, and the more trauma to which the child was exposed.

There are some people who, as infants, had a relatively low-sensitivity temperament and whose sentitivity was bumped up into the 'average' range through exposure to traumatic events early in life. In these cases, there is a good chance of these people will lead a normal happy life if they are able to work through the issues associated with the trauma.

However, it is a very different story if the child began with a high-sensitivity temperament. Children whose sensitivity was genetically set at a high level at birth, and who then experienced traumatic events early in life which increased their sensitivity further, will face many more emotional challenges in adulthood than those who started with a low-sensitivity temperament.

Interestingly, the type of abuse which affects sensitivity is different between boys and girls. Boys will tend to be affected much more by neglect than physical abuse, whereas girls are affected much more by physical abuse than neglect. Nevertheless, in both boys and girls, the effects of neglect and abuse is a disruption in a specific portion of the *corpus colossum* – the structure in the brain that connects the two halves, or hemispheres, of the brain together. This disruption in the corpus colossum results in an increase in emotional volatility, distractibility and self-destructive behavior.

The purpose of discussing the effect of early childhood trauma on your sensitivity is to help you begin to answer the question for yourself "Why Do I Keep Doing That?" When you have a high-sensitivity temperament, you feel differently and act differently from people with a low-sensitivity temperament. It is important that you don't feel bad about who you are, but rather try to understand and embrace the unique challenges your particular degree of sensitivity creates.

For many years of my life, I felt like there was something wrong with me because I could not act like other kids my age. While those around me could study, complete projects, play sports and had a lot of friends, I was lucky to be able to just sit at my desk. I could not concentrate, focus my attention or stick with any one thing long enough to accomplish it. By the time I was in the sixth grade, the school put me through a battery of tests to find out whether I even had the academic skills to be at my current grade level. Even though the tests came back that my problem solving abilities were the equivalent of a high school senior when I was only in the sixth grade, I eventually graduated from high school with only a 1.7 grade point average.

My problem was that because of my high-sensitivity, I could not muster the ability to control my emotions or actions well enough to take advantage of the gifts I had been given. If I had understood the source of the problem, I could have taken action to change it and savied years of suffering from the wrath of frustrated parents and teachers, and thinking that there was something wrong with me.

High Sensitivity and Emotional Hijackings

An *emotional hijacking* is when your emotions become so intense and overwhelming that they take control over your actions. Under the bondage of an emotional hijacking, you will tend to do things which are self-destructive and lead to frustration and unhappiness. The number of times I have personally experienced these hijackings is too numerous to count. Under the bondage of emotional hijackings I have gone on huge spending sprees, I have smashed things like awards, electronic equipment and furniture in fits of rage, I have engaged in angry shouting matches with co-workers, and have said many hurtful and cruel things toward people I love. Even at the time, I hated doing these things. After each emotional hijacking, I was sickened to think about how I had acted. Even today, when I look back at the things I have done, I shudder to think that was me. However, today I understand what was driving that behavior. It was not that I was a bad person. It was that I was under the influence of emotions which I could not control.

People are inherently good. Although many people act in bad ways, it is usually not their intent to do so, but rather it is the result of emotional hijackings. Emotional hijackings are almost always driven by negative emotions because, as you learned in the last chapter, negative emotions are stronger than positive emotions. Consequently, if you are going to lose control due to being overwhelmed by your emotions, it will most likely be the negative emotions that push you over the edge.

One exception to this is if you suffer from bipolar disorder; what is sometimes called manic-depression. When you have bipolar, there will be a period where you feel super – the mania phase – followed by a period where you feel horrible – the depression phase. While in the mania phase, you often experience an emotional hijacking by your positive emotions. You may become convinced that you are super-important and loved by everyone, you may feel super powerful and believe you can do anything.

Whether your emotional hijacking is from positive or negative emotions, the hijacking occurs when your emotional centers are stimulated so much that the emotions take over control of your behavior. This is more likely to happen if you have a high-sensitivity temperament simply because of the increased emotional intensity you experience.

In a workshop on emotions I gave recently, I had everyone in the room take the Sensitivity Test found at the end of this chapter. As expected, every single person in the room had a high-sensitivity temperament. Those with a low-sensitivity temperament, who don't experience emotions very intensely, generally do not struggle with overwhelming negative emotions like the high-sensitivity types do, and are not very likely to seek out answers for why they keep acting and feeling the way they do. That is not to say that those with a low-sensitivity temperament don't suffer from negative emotions. It is just that those negative emotions tend to not have the degree of intensity necessary to create an emotional hijacking. On the other hand, most people who have a high-sensitivity desperately want to learn how to free themselves from the overwhelming negative emotions and the frequent emotional hijackings they experience.

The Beauty of a High-Sensitivity Temperament

So far, we have talked a lot about the negative parts about having a high-sensitivity temperament. But it is not all bad. As a matter of fact, now that I have been able to free myself from the bondage of negative emotions, I wouldn't trade my high-sensitivity temperament for anything. Here is why:

- With a high-sensitivity temperament you experience emotions very intensely. This means that once you get rid of the negative emotions, the intensity of joy, empowerment and other positive emotions is awesome. You feel like your life is full of meaning, passion and purpose.
- With a high-sensitivity temperament your senses are heightened, allowing you to experience life more sensually. You can find more pleasure in pampering the senses with music, food, art, smells and touch.
- With a high-sensitivity temperament you are much more emotionally available and aware, which gives you the ability to form deeply intimate and meaningful relationships and to have more empathy for others.
- With a high-sensitivity temperament your ability to see things and sense things which others cannot gives you a heightened degree of creativity.

The vast majority of artists, writers and musicians have a high-sensitivity temperament.

A high-sensitivity temperament is like a double-edged sword. On one side if your emotions are largely negative, the emotional intensity can cut your life to ribbons. On the other side, when you eliminate the negative emotional hijackings by changing the emotions you experience, you can live a life which is intensely wonderful.

Sensitivity and Relationships

Because people vary so much in where they fall on the sensitivity continuum, rarely do both partners in a relationship to have the same degree of sensitivity. This means that in all likelihood, you have either a higher or a lower degree of sensitivity than your partner does. This is not necessarily a bad thing, it just means that there will be a difference in how emotional you are in comparison to your partner.

If you are a high-sensitivity type and your partner is a low-sensitivity type, you will likely feel that your partner is not as emotionally available as you would like. You may also feel that they don't communicate their feelings enough and they don't notice when you are upset like they should. You will be the one who usually initiates heart-to-heart talks and will often feel frustrated when your partner doesn't seem to take them as seriously as you do.

On the other hand, if you are the low-sensitivity partner, you will often feel as though your high-sensitivity partner wallows in emotion too much and that they are too melodramatic. You will likely feel as though your partner expects you to just somehow "know" that they are upset, as though you are some kind of mind-reader, and wish that they would stop "reading into" your actions things which you feel are not true.

A mismatch in sensitivity type can make for an interesting and comical relationship as long as both partners understand the other's sensitivity. If you can develop a sense of humor about how emotional you are or how non-emotional your partner is, and not judge one way as being better than the other, you will be able to work toward eliminating a major source of frustration that a lot of couples experience.

To Sum Up About Sensitivity

In this chapter you learned that sensitivity is the intensity with which you experience your emotions. If you have a high-sensitivity temperament, you will tend to experience your emotions and senses very intensely. If you have a low-sensitivity temperament, you will tend to have a muted sense of emotion and will require an excess of sensory stimulation to feel what the average person feels. This variability in sensitivity is created through a combination of your genetics and the events you experienced during your first few years of life. Once your sensitivity has become established, it does not change over your lifetime. Since your degree of sensitivity controls the intensity with which you experience emotions, the higher your sensitivity is, the more important it is for you to eliminate negative emotions.

Exercise

What is Your Sensitivity Temperament?

~~~~~~~~~~~~~~~~

In this exercise, you will be able to determine whether you have a high-sensitivity temperament, a low-sensitivity temperament or a temperament somewhere in between. As you discovered in this chapter, your degree of sensitivity has a big impact on your emotional volatility and intensity. By the end of this exercise, you will have a better idea of where you fall on the sensitivity continuum.

Your Sensitivity Temperament - Part 1

The Questionnaire

In the short questionnaire which follows you will be presented with a series of paired statements. Next to each statement in the pair is a box. For each pair, check the box next to the statement which is more true for you right now. For example, if you see yourself as more of a cat person, than a dog person you would place an "X" in the box which corresponds to the statement:

4)   A) ❏ I see myself as more of a cat person.
       B) ☒ I see myself as more of a dog person.

---

1)   A) ❏ I tend to feel things very intensely.
       B) ❏ I am not a very emotional person.

2)   A) ❏ I am typically not bothered by loud and busy events.
       B) ❏ I tend to shy away from loud and busy events.

3)   A) ❏ I am rarely distracted by ambient sounds.
       B) ❏ I am often distracted by ambient sounds.

4)   A) ❏ I see myself as more of a cat person.
       B) ❏ I see myself as more of a dog person.

5)   A) ❏ It is often difficult for me to finish a project I have started.
       B) ❏ I finish just about everything that I start.

6) A) ❑ I often feel that I can sense things that others can't.
   B) ❑ I don't consider myself more sensitive than average.

7) A) ❑ I prefer hobbies that are fast and intense.
   B) ❑ I prefer hobbies that are more subdued and quiet.

8) A) ❑ I have had an anxiety or panic attack.
   B) ❑ I have never had an anxiety or panic attack.

9) A) ❑ I tend to be more of an intellectual type.
   B) ❑ I tend to be more of a passionate type.

10) A) ❑ I can handle many tasks without becoming stressed.
    B) ❑ I often become stressed when I have to handle many tasks.

11) A) ❑ I see myself as unusually observant.
    B) ❑ I see myself as no more observant than average.

12) A) ❑ I don't know when someone is upset unless they tell me.
    B) ❑ I can usually sense when someone else is upset.

13) A) ❑ I would rather work with people.
    B) ❑ I would rather work away from other people.

14) A) ❑ I frequently find it difficult to relax.
    B) ❑ I have no trouble calming myself down.

15) A) ❑ My thoughts are typically organized and calm.
    B) ❑ My mind is typically racing with thoughts.

Your Sensitivity Temperament - Part 2

Tally Your Answers

For each column below, go to the question number listed and mark down whether you had selected 'A' or 'B.' Then tally the total for each column. Note that not all of the questions you answered count toward your final score. The sample on the left is an example of how to tally your answers:

Q #	(HS)	(LS)		Q #	(HS)	(LS)
1	~~A~~	B		1	A	B
2	~~B~~	A		2	B	A
3	~~B~~	A		3	B	A
5	A	~~B~~		5	A	B
6	~~A~~	B		6	A	B
7	B	~~A~~		7	B	A
8	A	~~B~~		8	A	B
10	~~B~~	A		10	B	A
11	~~A~~	B		11	A	B
12	B	~~A~~		12	B	A
14	~~A~~	B		14	A	B
15	~~B~~	A		15	B	A
Total:	8	4		Total:		

Your Sensitivity Temperament - Part 3

Figure Your Score

From each of the columns that you tallied above, place the number in the space below which corresponds to the total tallied on the previous page. For example:

(HS) __8__ -(LS) __4__ = __4__ Sensitivity Score

On the lines below, enter your numbers from the previous page and calculate your Sensitivity Score:

(HS) _____ -(LS) _____ = _____ Sensitivity Score

Plot Your Answers On the Sensitivity Continuum

Using the information calculated above, mark your answers on the appropriate spot on the line below.

Low-Sensitivity   High-Sensitivity

-7 -6 -5 -4 -3 -2 -1   0   1   2   3   4   5   6   7

Sensitivity Continuum

Your Sensitivity Temperament - Part 4

How Does Your Temperament Help Explain Your Experience with Emotions?

Whether you scored high or low on the sensitivity continuum, write a few lines about how you think your degree of sensitivity may contribute to your daily experience with emotions:

_____

_____

_____

_____

_____

_____

_____

_____

_____

Chapter 3

The Emotional Memory Loop

~~~~~~~~~~~~~~~~

So far you have learned about your four subconscious perceptions, how those four subconscious perceptions stimulate the two emotional centers in the brain to create eight primary emotions and how your sensitivity is responsible for the intensity with which you feel your emotions. In this chapter, you will go one step further and learn about *emotional memories* and how your emotional memories create your moods and the din of chatter that goes through your mind throughout the day. Once you understand how an emotional memory loop is set up, you will have a powerful tool that you can use to change how you feel and what you think about throughout the day.

Three Types of Memory

Since this chapter is about emotional memory, let's start out by defining other types of memory – factual and procedural – and by describing how emotional memory differs from these.

Factual Memory

Factual memory is how you remember facts. A factual memory would include anything that someone could tell you or that you could learn from a book. Your phone number is a fact, as are multiplication tables, names of historical figures, your address or a work of fiction. Factual memories are stored in the conscious mind.

The nice thing about factual memories is that you can change it quickly and easily – all you have to do is just read something or learn something new. The drawback is that your ability to retain factual memories is very limited, compared to your ability to retain procedural and emotional memories. Factual memories are only stored for a short time and are easily forgotten.

Procedural Memory

Procedural memory is how you remember actions. This differs from factual memory in that you can't learn it from a book, you can only develop procedural memory by doing something. For example, you could read books on how to ride a bicycle, but all of the facts about riding a bicycle won't help you much when you try to ride. The only way to learn how to ride a bicycle is to get on and pedal. No matter how much you know, you will still fall a few times. But once you get the hang of it, you can ride all day long without even having to concentrate on it.

One of the differences between factual memory and procedural memory is that in order to access a factual memory, like a phone number, you have to focus your attention on it. Whereas with procedural memory, you don't have to think about it at all. Where your factual memory is stored in your conscious mind, your procedural memory is stored in the subconscious.

Because procedural memory and factual memory operate separately, you can knit while carrying on a conversation, or play guitar and sing at the same time. You can do two things at once because your factual memory and your procedural memory use two different levels of your mind. Neither level can do two things at once, but since your subconscious operates pretty much independently from your conscious, each level can do one thing while the other level does something else.

The subconscious stores memories much longer than the conscious mind, so once you develop a procedural memory, you don't forget it as quickly. As with the example of riding a bicycle. Once you develop the procedural memory of riding a bicycle, it is stored for a long time.

Emotional Memory

Emotional memory is a special type of memory made up of two parts: emotions and facts. Whenever you experience an emotional reaction to an event, your subconscious mind will pull up other memories with a similar emotional theme. If you are feeling fear, your mind will recall other situations where you experienced fear.

Like all other aspects of emotion, emotional memory is also an important survival mechanism. It is a way for the mind to hasten your reaction to an event. Instead of having to think about what you are going to do in any given emotional circumstance, your mind pulls up other events that have the same emotional content and replays them. From these emotional memories, the mind is trying to find how you responded to a similar situation before.

As stated, an emotional memory has two parts: an emotional part and a factual part. Even though the emotional part is stored in the subconscious

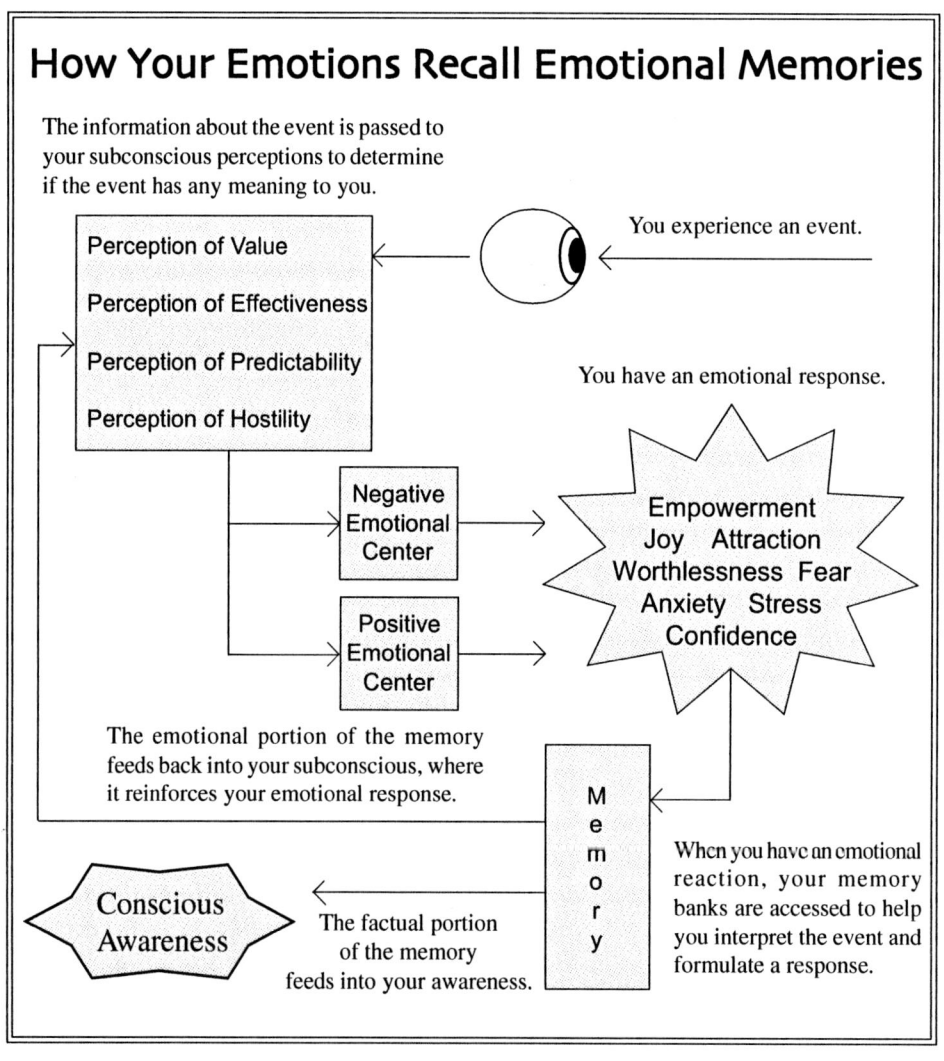

mind and the factual part is stored in the conscious mind, the two parts are tethered together so that when you recall one part, you recall both.

The problem is that since the conscious mind does not store memories as well as the subconscious mind stores them, over time details surrounding a particular situation will become fuzzy and faint. Most people are able to recall the feeling of being at the fair, being with their grandparents or being in school when they were young. These are emotional memories. However, most people will not be able to recall many of the details of that time - the clothes people were wearing, what day of the week it was - because these details are stored in the conscious mind. Since the conscious mind does not store memories as long as the subconscious mind, most of the facts will have been lost, but the feeling will remain.

This degradation of the factual portion of the emotional memory may be so complete that at times your mind will not be able to recall any of the details of what actually happened. All that you will be able to recall is the emotional part. You may have a kind of haunting emotional feeling when you smell an aroma that reminds you of something in your past; a vague memory that you just can't quite recall.

Filling In the Gaps

One of the truths about the human mind is that it likes consistency. Your mind will try to make your memory of the details of an event consistent with your emotions of the event. When you experience a particular emotion, your mind will selectively filter out the details which are inconsistent with the emotion you experience and only store those details which are consistent. If you forget some of the details of an event, your conscious mind will set out to "fill in the gaps" and rebuild a scenario which is consistent with the emotional portion of the memory. Because of this, you will have memories, especially from when you were younger, that are an amalgam of a few factual details and your own imagination. Now this is where emotional memories really get interesting.

Since your mind likes consistency and will filter out details which are inconsistent with the emotion, and since any gaps in the details of your experience will be filled in by your conscious mind for consistency, *your emotions influence the creation of facts to justify and reinforce themselves.* Certainly you have had a disagreement with someone else over the details of a shared event. Both of you were probably equally certain that your own version of the event was correct.

The story that I told in Chapter One about the sales meeting I was in with a co-worker of mine illustrates this phenomenon perfectly. The bottom line was that she and I sat in the same room, listened to the same words, were asked the same questions, even drank the same coffee, but her experience was very different than mine. Because she felt threatened by the management and I didn't, she filtered out many of the details which conflicted with her emotion of fear. Consequently, by the end of the meeting, she had collected enough evidence in her mind to prove to herself that she was being attacked. A couple of days later, she brought up the situation again and began describing details of the meeting which just did not happen. Her conscious mind used her imagination to create details to justify her emotional state.

When your imagination is used to create details which are consistent with your emotional state, your conscious mind is actually reinforcing the emotion you are experiencing.

Phantom Events

What happens when you recall an emotional memory and all of the details of the memory are lost? You experience what I call a *phantom event*.

A phantom event is an image or situation which is completely fabricated in your mind, and which is consistent with the emotion you are experiencing. These form spontaneously and are completely unpredictable. For example, one day I was walking out of a retail store into the warmth of the mid-afternoon sun. It was early summer and all of the trees were in full bloom filling the air with their perfume. As I stepped through the front door of the store a strong image filled my head of someone jumping out of the bushes and viciously stabbing me over and over again. By the time I walked to my car, the image was gone. "What was that all about?" I thought. What I had experienced was a phantom event.

One of the negative emotions I struggled with for many years was fear. I felt fear of people all the time, sometimes to a greater degree than others. On this particular day, I had felt an ill-defined emotional unrest that I couldn't quite put my finger on. It wasn't very intense, but I felt like something was wrong. The phantom event of someone jumping out of the bushes and attacking me was my conscious mind's way of justifying the emotion I was experiencing. Any emotion can create a phantom event, but since negative emotions are more intense than positive emotions, phantom events tend to be negative.

One last thing on phantom events: Phantom events are responsible for the phenomenon of recalled repressed memories. You have probably heard about adults recalling memories of abuse from their childhood during therapy. Some people have been convicted and were sent to prison based on the recalled repressed memory testimony. Eventually many of these convictions were overturned because it was discovered that the alleged events could not have occurred as recalled by the plaintiff.

This is not to say that childhood abuse did not occur to these people. On the contrary, there was very likely a history of abuse which left them with very intense emotional memories. Unfortunately, as time passed, the details were lost and all that remained were the powerful emotions of fear, anxiety and worthlessness associated with the abuse. In most cases, recalling those details is next to impossible. Instead, the conscious mind constructs mental images of what must have happened to justify the emotions. Because these phantom events are created in response to the emotions, the phantom events will feel very real.

Now that you have learned about emotional memories and how they can create phantom events, let's take a look at another phenomenon associated with emotional memories – the *emotional memory loop*.

The Emotional Memory Loop

So far, you have learned that events in your life, especially early in life, are responsible for creating your perceptions about yourself and about your world. You learned that those perceptions are stored in your subconscious mind and that they control which emotions you experience. You learned that when you experience an emotion you will recall emotional memories, and that the factual details associated with these emotional memories may not be able to be recalled completely. You learned that when details are missing from an emotional event, the conscious mind will use your imagination to create a scenario which is consistent with the emotion you are experiencing, and that this scenario will feel very real, even when it is not.

When emotional memories are recalled, the emotional part of the memory will be experienced by the subconscious as a new emotional experience. Because your subconscious perceptions are created through experiencing emotional events, the emotional memory will reinforce the perception which created the emotion in the first place. So, your subconscious perceptions stimulate an emotion, the emotion triggers the recall of emotional memories with a similar theme, the emotional memory is experienced by the subconscious as a new emotional event and reinforces the perception that began the whole process. In this way, emotional memories create a loop between an emotion and the perception which created it. The accompanying schematic illustrates how this whole process works.

The remaining pages of this chapter focus on how the emotional memory loop affects your mood, what you think about during the day and

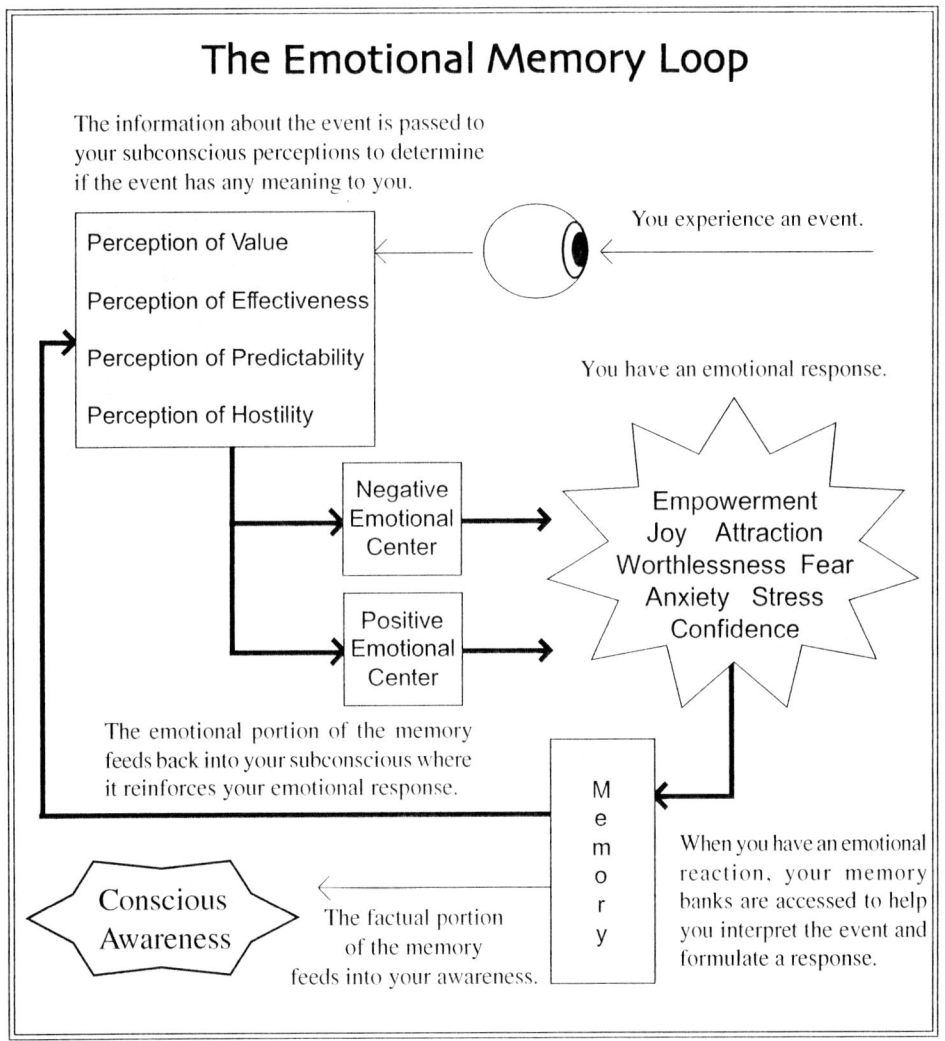

how you act. This will be followed by a discussion about how the emotional memory loop becomes a very powerful source of bondage to a particular pattern of feeling, thinking and acting. Finally, you will learn how to use phantom events as one of three techniques for using the emotional memory loop to change your perceptions, and hence, how you feel, think and act.

The Emotional Memory Loop Creates Your Mood

Your mood is set by the pattern of emotions you experience throughout the day. If the emotions you experience are primarily positive ones, like joy and confidence, your mood will be good; you will feel happy and calm. If the emotions you experience are primarily negative ones, like worthlessness and anxiety, your mood will not be so good; you will feel depressed and anxious. It is not necessary for anything bad to happen to you in order to have a bad day. If you are like I was, you may have days where everything is going just fine, but you still feel bad.

Your emotional memory loop sets your mood in the following way: From the time you get up in the morning until the time you go to bed at night, you are experiencing small events, such as finding your keys to get into your car, interacting with your partner, children or co-workers, driving in traffic or standing in line to get a cup of coffee. To most of these events, you will have an emotional reaction. Most of the emotional reactions you have are very small reactions, but they are emotional reactions just the same. Each one of these small emotions activates your emotional memory loop and you re-experience the emotions of past experiences that had a similar emotional theme. If your perceptions are such that you tend to react positively, your emotional memory loop will begin to replay positive emotional memories. But if you are like most people, the opposite is true. Your perceptions stimulate negative emotions and so you recall and re-live negative emotional memories.

Keep in mind that you may not be consciously aware that this is happening. Because most of the processing of emotional memories occurs in the subconscious, you aren't directly aware that they are being retrieved. One of the ways that you can keep tabs on what emotional memories are being recalled is to pay attention to the conscious part of the emotional memory – the details or facts – which run through your mind. This conscious factual part of the emotional memory is usually experienced as a quick subtle image, a fragment of a conversation or a comment someone made to you. This din of conscious activity which plays out in your awareness is what are called *automatic thoughts.*

The Emotional Memory Loop Generates Your Automatic Thoughts

Automatic thoughts are just that – automatic. They appear all by themselves. You can't directly control them because they are pulled into the conscious mind when an emotional memory is recalled in the subconscious. The intensity of the automatic thought is in direct proportion to the intensity of the emotional memory. In turn, the intensity of the emotional memory is in direct proportion to the intensity of the emotion which triggered the emotional memory in the first place. Since your emotions are generated based on your subconscious perceptions of your self and your world, your automatic thoughts are going to be experienced in a manner that is consistent with your subconscious perceptions.

For many years I had a very low perception of value and felt pretty much worthless and depressed all of the time. Each day, interspersed with thoughts like "where are my socks?" or "where can I come up with five bucks for gas?" my mind was filled with thoughts like this:

Image: Everyone standing around at my funeral, following my suicide, feeling really, really bad that they didn't care about me and didn't listen to me when they had the chance. I feel a sense of revenge for making them finally realize how much they screwed up.

Thought: "If my girlfriend really loved me, then she would change her schedule so that she could see me every day."

Feeling: Sudden strong urge to run. I need to go somewhere.

Thought: "I am so sick of people always taking advantage of me and treating me like crap. Don't they know who I am?"

Image: Being trapped in a submarine that was filling with water.

Thought: "If my dad cared about me at all, then he would make some time to spend with me."

Thought: "Normal people don't feel bad like this – I must just be a loser by nature."

Image: Being attacked by a vicious gang, having my abdomen cut open and my guts pulled out onto the street.

These disturbing automatic thoughts were all ultimately created by my perception that I was worthless, that my life was out of control, and that the world was hostile and dangerous. The suicidal thoughts were driven by the emotion of worthlessness associated with my low perception of value

Cognitive Distortions Associated with Depression

Excerpt from: *Feeling Good: The New Mood Therapy* by David Burns

Dr. David Burns was one of the early champions of a branch of psychology called Cognitive-Behavioral Therapy, along with Aaron Beck. In Dr. Burns' book, *Feeling Good*, he describes a number of common "congnitive distortions" or abnormal ways of thinking in people who suffer from depression. All of these distortions arise out of subconscious perceptions and the emotional memory loop.

1) **All-or-nothing thinking.** If your performance falls short of perfect, you see yourself as a total failure.

2) **Overgeneralization.** You see a single negative event as a never-ending pattern of defeat.

3) **Mental filter.** You pick out a single negative detail and dwell on it exclusively so that your entire vision of reality becomes darkened.

4) **Disqualifying the positive.** You reject positive experiences by insisting that they don't count for some reason or other.

5) **Emotional reasoning.** You assume that your negative emotions necessarily reflect the way things really are: "I feel it, therefore it must be true."

6) **Personalization.** You see yourself as the cause of some negative external event which, in fact, you were not primarily responsible for.

and the anxiety associated with feeling like I had no control over my life. The recurrent image of being trapped in a sinking submarine and being attacked by a vicious gang were both phantom events created by the anxiety associated with the perception of being out of control, coupled with the fear associated with the perception that the world was hostile.

There was one thing in common with all of the negative thoughts which made up my daily mental life for many years: *I hated them all.* But I didn't believe that there was any alternative for me. I thought that I was just one of the statistical few who was a loser, was mentally incapable of being normal and had no hope of accomplishing anything. I was so unhappy, and to have an endless rapid-fire of disturbing images and thoughts racing through my mind was so fatiguing that after a while, death seemed to be the only thing that offered relief.

Today I can see the humor and absurdity in the automatic thoughts I had. But that is only because they are no longer part of my day. I certainly did not think they were funny at the time.

Automatic thoughts are vitally important because they provide very important information about the emotional memories being recalled and about the condition of the underlying perceptions. The important points to discussion from this discussion are:

- Your automatic thoughts are the factual part of your emotional memories.
- Your ability to recall factual memory is very limited.
- Your mind fills in the gaps in your factual memory with what seems to be consistent with the emotion of the memory.
- In some cases, your conscious mind has to completely fabricate a 'factual' scenario to match the emotion you are feeling – a phantom event.
- Because the automatic thoughts and phantom events are linked to an emotion, they feel real, even when they are not.

Or put in another way: *You can't always believe everything you think!*

The Emotional Memory Loop Affects Your Decisions and Actions

I volunteered for a time at the Sexual Violence Center of Minneapolis. While I was there, a woman called in who had been sexually assaulted over the weekend and wanted to speak to a counselor. She had been hitchhiking alone, on a remote stretch of highway, just before one o'clock in the morning when she was picked up by a stranger and assaulted. The fact that she was hitchhiking by no stretch meant that she was *'asking for it'* in any way, but I had to wonder why someone would put themselves in that kind of vulnerable position knowing that there was a chance that some violent creep would stop and pick her up. What amazed me was that this was actually the third time that she had been sexually assaulted in the past six months on that same road while hitchhiking alone in the middle of the night. Each time, the experience was horrifying for her. "My God!" I thought. "Why would someone keep doing that, in spite of being hurt repeatedly?"

The tragedy of this woman's story was that as a consequence of her decisions, she often put herself in a very vulnerable situation; a situation where she could get hurt. Although this was never her intent, she did not make the connection that her decision to hitchhike alone in the middle of the night could result in her being harmed. But before judging her decisions too harshly, I would suggest that, without realizing it, you too make decisions which leave you in a position to be hurt or suffer hardship.

Sometimes bad decisions are just made out of inexperience. When you suffer consequences because of inexperience, you are able to learn from them and avoid making the bad decision again. Any time you start a new job, begin a new relationship or take up a new hobby, you have to learn how to navigate through a new set of rules. Many of these rules are discovered through trial and error. Over time, you get the knack of what you need to do and you don't make as many mistakes. However, when the same mistakes are made repeatedly, and the same consequences are experienced again and again, you have to suspect that negative subconscious perceptions are the culprit.

One of my patterns of bad decisions involving negative subconscious perceptions revolved around money. The whole process went something like this:

- I had a low perception of value which made me feel bad about myself.
- One of the automatic thoughts that would pop into my head was that people who were successful and felt good about themselves were able to buy nice things.
- A quick phantom event would run through my mind where I was buying something nice and I felt valued and empowered; like I had arrived at my success and everyone thought I was really something special.
- The next thing I knew, I was looking at expensive clothes, jewelry, cameras and cars. All of the attention that I received made me feel special, and at least for that moment, I felt like a king. I loved to think about the fact that for all the sales person knew, I was someone really rich and successful.
- I felt like I had to pretend like money wasn't an issue. I thought that if I appeared to flinch at a price tag, that the sales person would realize that I was a fraud and my façade would come crashing down. I so much didn't want to leave my little bubble that I stayed and played the part of the big spender as long as I could.
- Eventually, I drove home with new merchandise that I couldn't afford

and began the long process of trying to figure out how I could justify what I had just done. I began to rehearse lines that I would use on my wife to make her think that this purchase was a good idea – or even better, a necessity. That's it! It was necessary! I had to have it! It would have been irresponsible for me to not buy it!
- Then came the solemn day of figuring out how much money we had to pay bills, and the realization that the money that was spent on superfluous stuff meant that we could not pay our mortgage.
- This was followed by a stern resolution never to do it again. I felt so horrible about my inability to control my spending behavior that it further undermined my perception of value, and so the pattern continued.

Although the specifics in your case may be slightly different, this pattern is pretty typical for people addicted to spending, gambling, having extramarital affairs, or overeating. In this instance, I use the word addiction to mean "repeatedly engaging in any activity which ultimately creates unhappiness, and being unable or unwilling to stop." The only way to break out of this pattern is to change the perceptions that lead to the poor decisions in the first place.

The Emotional Memory Loop is the Source of Emotional Bondage

Since your emotional memories are ultimately created by your subconscious perceptions, your experience of reality is entirely directed by those perceptions. For example, if you have the perception that you are not valued, you will feel worthless, your automatic thoughts will reinforce your worthlessness with a mixture of actual events and phantom events, and you will behave in various ways to create events in your life which will further support your perception of worthlessness.

This phenomenon is like *emotional bondage*, where the perceptions you hold about yourself and about the world around you control your feelings, thoughts and actions in such a way as to make your perceptions become reality. Because your perceptions exist in the subconscious and the emotional memory loops take place in the subconscious, this bondage happens whether or not you are even aware of it.

Abraham Lincoln is credited with saying that "people are as happy as they make their mind up to be." Although President Lincoln was certainly a gifted statesman, he didn't understand the power of subconscious perceptions. How many times have you made up your mind to be happier, more successful, thinner, healthier or more financially responsible? What usually happened? If you are like most people, you probably had some success for a time, but eventually you fell back into your old behavior. If you were brave, you made another commitment to work even harder and tried again. The problem is that very little can be changed by willpower alone. You must understand how your perceptions create an emotional bondage which keeps you at a certain place, how to break free from your current emotional bondage and how to create a new emotional bondage which keeps you locked in a happy, passionate and successful life. The key to turning your life in a new direction rests upon one single thing: changing your perceptions.

Changing Your Perceptions by Changing Your Emotional Memory Loop

The key to changing how you feel, think and act is to change your perceptions. There is no way that you can directly reprogram your perceptions. You can, however, indirectly reprogram your perceptions through changing your emotional memory loop. You can do this by taking advantage of a number of things: your mind's need for consistency, your subconscious ability to respond emotionally to phantom events, and the fact that your actions can create emotional responses. Let's take a quick look at each one of these.

Your Mind's Need for Consistency

One of the realities about your mind is that it is always striving for consistency. It wants your behavior, thoughts and feelings to be consistent with your perceptions of the world and your place in it. Once these perceptions are established at around four or five years of age, you will spend the rest of their lives having your thoughts, feelings and behavior directed by these perceptions.

Well, there is some good news and some bad news about this. The good news is that not only will your perceptions direct your thoughts, feelings and behavior, but your thoughts, feelings and behavior will also direct your perceptions. This means that if you can change what you think, what you feel and how you act, you can change your perceptions. Let me explain what I mean by this.

As we have talked about in this chapter, when you experience an emotional event, your emotional memory loop kicks in and begins pulling up emotional memories and generating automatic thoughts. You have the ability to create an image in your mind which will stimulate an emotional response, right? Surely you can visualize some image or situation where you feel valued or empowered. This will stimulate the emotional memory loop to recall similar positive emotional memories and since your mind likes consistency, your perceptions will begin to change to be consistent with the emotions that are being generated. It turns out that you can also change your behavior and change your thoughts to create the same effect on your perceptions.

The bad news is that when you try to reverse the process from having your perceptions control your emotional memory loop to purposely controlling your emotional memory loop to change your perceptions, you will experience a strange sense of disorientation. You may feel like you are being phony, like you are acting like someone you are not; and you are right. Your are not acting like who you are, but rather like who you want to become. This strange feeling of disorientation will be experienced whenever you change from a *reactive* emotional memory loop to a *proactive* emotional memory loop.

Fortunately, you only have to experience the feeling of disorientation while you are changing your perceptions. Once your perceptions are reprogrammed, you will have reset the emotional memory loop and it will maintain itself there pretty well on its own.

Your Subconscious Ability to Respond Emotionally to Phantom Events

A quiet din of sniffles filled the theater while Bette Midler sang *Wind Beneath My Wings* in the movie *Beaches*. Even though everyone in the theater consciously knew that no one had really died, people were still moved to tears because someone pretended to die. Music, movies, dance, opera, fine art, literature – all of these things move us emotionally, but they are not real events; they are phantom events. But we react emotionally to phantom events as though they were real events.

Just as our mind may create a phantom event when an emotional memory is recalled, we can also purposely create a phantom event which will recall an emotional memory. This emotional memory is then experienced by the subconscious as though it were a real event and will therefore reinforce a perception which is consistent with the emotion. If you purposely create a positive phantom event in your mind, and you concentrate on it and visualize every detail of it, you will improve the emotions you experience.

Your Actions Can Create Emotional Responses

We have talked quite a bit about how your emotions can drive your behavior. The opposite is also true: your behavior can drive your emotions. Each time you experience an event, it affects your subconscious perceptions. This is true even if you purposely create an event through your actions. Remember from Introduction that the subconscious mind cannot differentiate truth from fiction? This characteristic of the subconscious mind is easy to exploit to create a positive change in your perceptions. All you have to do is act as if you were valued and empowered and your subconscious perceptions will begin to form in that way.

If you suffer from fear, all you have to do is purposely act as though you were not afraid; take some risks and become more emotionally vulnerable to others. You can even hand pick the person with whom you are going to do this. You can tell them how to respond to you and what you want them to say. It doesn't matter if you orchestrate the whole situation. Your subconscious won't know the difference, and will treat the event in the same fashion as it would a real event.

To Sum Up on the Emotional Memory Loop

In this chapter you learned about the three different types of memory: factual memory, procedural memory and emotional memory. You learned how emotional memories are actually comprised of two parts – a factual part, and an emotional part. The factual part of the emotional memory is stored in the conscious mind, whereas the emotional part of it is stored in the subconscious mind. You also learned about the fact that the conscious mind does not store memories as effectively as the subconscious. This results in deterioration of the factual part of the emotional memory.

You learned about your emotional memory loop and that the purpose of this loop is to reinforce your perceptions and create consistency between your feelings, thoughts and behaviors. You discovered how your emotional memory loop is responsible for generating your mood, your automatic thoughts and how these affect your behavior. You then learned how your emotional memory loop can also be used to reprogram your subconscious perceptions by purposefully creating phantom events and taking specific actions to improve these perceptions.

The next chapter is dedicated to teaching you how to use phantom events and purposeful symbolic action to change your emotional memory loop.

Exercise

Automatic Thoughts and Phantom Events

~~~~~~~~~~~~~~~~~~~~~~~~~

The purpose of this exercise is to increase your awareness of the influence your emotional memory loop has on your thoughts and behavior. For the next three days, write down one example of an automatic thought that you experience during the day and one example of a phantom event. In addition to writing down the thought or event, write down the emotions you felt at the time and exactly how you acted; what you did.

This exercise sounds simple, but may be hard to do. If you are like most people, you have become so accustomed to the automatic thoughts and phantom events that run through your mind, that you may have a hard time identifying them as such. Being able to identify them is a very important skill to develop because automatic thoughts and phantom events can be purposefully used as tools to change your emotional memory loop.

Automatic Thoughts and Phantom Events - Day 1

Situation: I was driving home from work

Phantom Event: An image of someone crashing into me and wrecking my car kept going through my mind

Secondary Emotion: I felt very nervous and guarded.

Primary Emotion: ☒ Fear ☐ Stress ☒ Anxiety ☐ Worthlessness
☐ Attraction ☐ Confidence ☐ Empowerment ☐ Joy

Actions I Took: I paid close attention to what everyone else was doing and drove very cautiously

---

Situation: I was waiting for my wife to get home. She was late.

Automatic Thought: For some reason I felt like I just knew that she had been in an accident and she was in trouble

Secondary Emotion: Scared and panicky.

Primary Emotion: ☒ Fear ☐ Stress ☒ Anxiety ☐ Worthlessness
☐ Attraction ☐ Confidence ☐ Empowerment ☐ Joy

Actions I Took: I kept checking the phone to see if she had called and looking out the window.

Automatic Thoughts and Phantom Events - Day 1

Situation: _____

Phantom Event: _____

_____

Secondary Emotion: _____

Primary Emotion: ☐ Fear   ☐ Stress   ☐ Anxiety   ☐ Worthlessness
                   ☐ Attraction   ☐ Confidence   ☐ Empowerment   ☐ Joy

Actions I Took: _____

Situation: _____

Automatic Thought: _____

_____

Secondary Emotion: _____

Primary Emotion: ☐ Fear   ☐ Stress   ☐ Anxiety   ☐ Worthlessness
                   ☐ Attraction   ☐ Confidence   ☐ Empowerment   ☐ Joy

Actions I Took: _____

Automatic Thoughts and Phantom Events – Day 2

Situation: _____

Phantom Event: _____

_____

Secondary Emotion: _____

Primary Emotion: ☐ Fear   ☐ Stress   ☐ Anxiety   ☐ Worthlessness
                  ☐ Attraction ☐ Confidence ☐ Empowerment ☐ Joy

Actions I Took: _____

Situation: _____

Automatic Thought: _____

_____

Secondary Emotion: _____

Primary Emotion: ☐ Fear   ☐ Stress   ☐ Anxiety   ☐ Worthlessness
                  ☐ Attraction ☐ Confidence ☐ Empowerment ☐ Joy

Actions I Took: _____

Automatic Thoughts and Phantom Events - Day 3

Situation: _____

Phantom Event: _____

_____

Secondary Emotion: _____

Primary Emotion: ☐ Fear   ☐ Stress   ☐ Anxiety   ☐ Worthlessness
                   ☐ Attraction   ☐ Confidence   ☐ Empowerment   ☐ Joy

Actions I Took: _____

Situation: _____

Automatic Thought: _____

_____

Secondary Emotion: _____

Primary Emotion: ☐ Fear   ☐ Stress   ☐ Anxiety   ☐ Worthlessness
                   ☐ Attraction   ☐ Confidence   ☐ Empowerment   ☐ Joy

Actions I Took: _____

Automatic Thoughts and Phantom Events - Day 4

Over the past three days, you have written down automatic thoughts and phantom events which have gone through your mind. You also wrote down what secondary and primary emotions you experienced. In this section, look back through what you have written to find patterns in the automatic thoughts you experienced and the phantom events you experienced and write down what you find.

Once you have written down the patterns you identified, think about an important question:

What primary and secondary emotions are the most common for you?

_____

_____

_____

_____

_____

_____

_____

Chapter 4

Three Facts, Eight Realities and Four Techniques of Change

In the first chapter, you learned about how your experiences early in life were used to form perceptions in your subconscious regarding your value as an individual, how much control you have over your environment, how hostile your environment is and how predictable your world is. These perceptions control the emotions you experience. So, to the same degree that your perceptions about yourself and your world are negative, you will experience negative emotions. On the other hand, when your perceptions are largely positive, you will experience positive emotions.

In the second chapter you learned about sensitivity and how that controls your emotional intensity. If you have a high-sensitivity temperament, you will experience emotions much more intensely than someone whose sensitivity is lower. The higher your degree of sensitivity, the greater your emotional intensity and the more your emotions drive your behavior. This means that the higher your degree of sensitivity, the more important it is to change your perceptions so that you experience positive emotions.

In the last chapter you learned about the phenomenon of the emotional memory loop, how emotions stimulate the recall of emotional memories and how these emotional memories serve to reinforce the perceptions which started the loop in the first place. You also learned that this whole process occurs in the subconscious mind, below your level of awareness.

In this chapter you will learn three facts about the subconscious mind which can be used to change the emotions you experience on a day-to-day basis. First, the subconscious mind cannot differentiate between real and imagined events. Second, the subconscious mind cannot differentiate between self and non-self. Third, your subconscious mind continuously tries to create consistency between what you perceive, what you think and feel and how you behave.

You will learn eight realities of changing your emotions. These are the realities that I have discovered through my own experience of emotional change as well as the experiences of those whom I have coached. This will be followed by four techniques to change the emotions you experience by changing your perceptions. These four simple techniques take advantage of the three facts unique to the subconscious mind and the eight realities of changing your emotions.

The Three Facts About the Subconscious Mind

Fact #1 – The Subconscious Mind Cannot Differentiate Between Real and Imagined Events

Why is it that you can go into a movie theater and be brought to tears by a movie that you consciously know is not real? Why is it that you can get yourself all upset by thinking about conversations or situations which have not even happened? Why is it that you get scared by telling ghost stories around the campfire? Why do you still feel afraid to do something even though you consciously know that there is nothing to be afraid of? It is simply because your subconscious perceptions, which generate your emotions, cannot differentiate between that which is true and that which is not true.

Understanding this lack of connection between reality and your emotional response is important for two reasons. First, you will tend to make decisions based on what feels real to you, not what is real. Many relationships have been damaged because one person believed something about the other person that, in fact was not true. Many dreams have never been realized because of the feeling that it just wasn't possible for those dreams to become reality.

Second, since imagined events can generate an emotional reaction just like real events, you can purposely create your own imagined events to change your emotional state. This can be done through visualization and meditation, or you can role-play scenarios with another person using scripted words and gestures. Even though your conscious mind knows that these events are not real, if you can get over feeling silly doing them and really get into it, your subconscious will experience these events as though they were real.

Fact #2 – The Subconscious Mind Cannot Differentiate Between Self and Non-Self

Your process of individuation, your awareness of yourself as an individual being separate and distinct from your parents and those around you, is the result of the development of the conscious mind. In your consciousness you are acutely aware of your separateness as a human being and you can easily differentiate yourself from those around you. However, the subconscious mind, where your emotions reside, does not make this distinction.

Your subconscious mind will emotionally respond to events outside of yourself as if they were happening to you. For example, how do you feel after watching a scary movie? Do you double-check to make sure your doors are locked? Do you jump when you hear a noise in your house after the lights are out? Do you experience the phantom events of a psycho-killer, a evil-possessed doll or some hidden alien monster actually being in your house or trying to get you? To some degree, we all feel this way.

How would you feel if you were walking down the street and you saw someone sitting on the curb crying? You would probably feel a little sad, right? How about if you are out with friends and they are laughing hysterically. Do you not start to chuckle even if you don't know what they are laughing at? Do you know someone who just seems to brighten everyone's spirits when they walk into the room? Have you ever met anyone with so much emotional intensity and passion that their behaviors, thoughts, goals and beliefs have an impact on yours?

Situations like these, where the emotions of other people and the events not involving us have the power to change our own emotional state occur because your subconscious mind cannot differentiate between what is happening to someone else and what is happening to you. Consciously you know the difference, but subconsciously your mind cannot separate self from non-self.

This phenomenon is the basis of empathy. Empathy is where you feel what another person feels. Empathy is critical for a couple of reasons. First, empathy is the main form of communication between an infant and his or her parents because infants cannot communicate in any other way. When they are uncomfortable, hungry, or frightened, all they can do is cry to communicate that something is upsetting them. Although the infant may not even be consciously aware of whethher they need food, sleep or a clean diaper because much of their conscious awareness has not developed, they are able to communicate to their parents, who through empathy are able to know what the infant needs.

Second, empathy is critical for relationships. In relationships, empathy is the ability to sense what the other person is feeling and being able to respond to their needs. It is the ability to put yourself in another person's position to feel how they feel. This ability allows the development of intimacy and understanding which are both critical for the formation of strong relationship bonds.

Lastly, since your subconscious uses your emotions in an effort to avoid hazards, you will respond emotionally to a situation where someone else was injured or killed. You will react to that event as though it had occurred to you and will attempt to avoid the situation as much as possible in the future. For example, if you read in the paper that an individual was robbed at gun-point while walking on Main Street, you will feel an aversion to walking on Main Street. If you do happen to walk down Main Street, you will feel uneasy and fearful as though you had been mugged there yourself.

The emotional response from empathy is certainly not as intense as the emotional response you would experience if the event actually occurred to you. But it is important to be aware that this phenomenon exists because of the influence it can have on your own emotional well-being. Later in this chapter you will learn how this aspect of your subconscious can be used to help change your perceptions.

Fact #3 – The Subconscious Mind Strives for Consistency Between Perceptions, Emotions, Thoughts and Actions

When I was in my early teens, the television show Charlie's Angels was a big hit and all of my friends had their eye on one of the Angels who they thought was hot. To make things even better, there were Charlie's Angels collector cards. Well, since I was only about 13 or 14 and had no money, I decided that in order to have my favorite Angel all to myself, I would just sneak a pack of the collector cards out of the local drug store. The first time I walked out of the store with a pack of Charlie's Angels collector cards, I felt almost sick with nervousness. I knew that I was doing something wrong and my emotions were racing. When I got out of the store without being caught, I rode my bike away as fast as my legs could pedal.

Soon after, I decided to go back again and take another pack of cards, then another, then another, and then another. Pretty soon, I no longer felt nervous or bad at all about stealing the cards. As a matter of fact, in a way I felt like the cards were really mine anyway and that the drug store was just holding them for me. I began stealing money from vending machines, stealing Slim Jims from the grocery store, and stealing toys from the local K-Mart. Before long, it seemed weird to me to actually pay for something.

Until I stole the first pack of cards, I had never stolen anything. I had grown up with the belief that stealing was bad and was only done by bad people. Consequently, the first time I did steal, I felt horrible. I felt bad because my actions were not in line with my perceptions and thoughts. But the more I acted in that particular way – the more I stole – the more my thoughts and perceptions changed to be in line with my actions and I felt less and less negative emotion when I took things that didn't belong to me.

This fact about the subconscious mind is what can keep you stuck in a self-destructive rut. When you try to change your actions, you may feel like I felt when I stole for the first time – like you are doing something wrong. This is true even if you are trying to do something positive. Your subconscious makes no moral judgement calls about what is right or wrong. It is interested in keeping your thoughts, perceptions, emotions and actions consistent. So, if you are afraid of people and you take the action to reach out to make some friends in spite of that fear, you will likely feel almost sick with anxiety and fear while you are doing it. But if you just take the action anyway, you will bump your thoughts and perceptions a little bit toward embracing other people. The more you take the action, the less you will respond negatively and the more natural it will become for you.

This aspect of your subconscious, along with the other two aspects listed above, can be used to reprogram your perceptions, and consequently, how you feel, think and act.

The Eight Realities of Changing Your Emotions

Reality #1 – Change Makes You Feel Disoriented

Your mind always tries maintain consistency between your perceptions, your thoughts, your feelings and your actions. Because of this, when you start changing what you think about and how you behave, your subconscious becomes a bit disoriented. Your subconscious has become so accustomed to your emotional memory loop generating the same pattern of thoughts, the same pattern of emotions and the same pattern of behavior, that when you try to change, your subconscious is thrust into foreign territory.

Changing your emotions is much like moving to a new city. You have to learn where everything is and how to get around, you have to meet new people, start a new job, and get used to your new house or apartment. All of this is stressful and disorienting. The reason why most people adapt successfully when they move to a new town, but struggle when trying to change their emotions is two-fold. First, when people move to a new town, they don't associate their feelings of disorientation and stress with doing something wrong. They expect to feel that way for a while when they move, so they try not to let those feelings interfere with getting used to a new environment.

When people try to change their emotions, they experience the same sort of disorientation and stress. But instead of expecting to experience those feelings as a natural consequence of change, as with moving, they interpret the feelings of disorientation and stress to mean that they are doing something wrong. Consequently, most people stop taking the action that was creating positive change in their life and quickly fall back into their old pattern of behavior.

The second reason why most people don't change is that they allow themselves an opportunity to quit. When you move to a new town, you no longer have the option of just moving back on a moment's notice – you are stuck there, and so you have to adapt to your new life. It is not so with deciding to make a change in your emotions and perceptions. You can just quit at any time and go back to the way you were.

One of the realities of changing your emotions is that you have to expect that you are going to feel disoriented and stressed. To expect anything else is unrealistic. You have to learn how to embrace those feelings, as uncomfortable as they may be, as a sign that you are beginning to change. The second side to this is that you must imagine that you have just been thrust into a new city with no option of moving back. If you think to yourself that you will just try changing your emotions for "a week or two and see what happens," you will not achieve any benefit. Changing your emotions requires a commitment that no matter how you feel, you will continue working toward a happier and more productive life.

Reality #2 – All That Matters is What You Do

One of the most important realities that I have learned through the years of changing my emotional life it is that *it doesn't matter what you feel, it doesn't matter what you think, all that matters is what you do.* Your mind will flop around like a fish out of water when you begin to change. That's a given. But just like a fish settles down once it is in a new tank of water, so will your mind. No matter how much the fish flops around while it is going through a tank change, all that matters is that you continue carrying it to its new home. The same is true with your mind. There is a temptation to allow your emotions to drive your behavior, especially when your emotions become intense and volatile. You subconscious mind tries to maintain consistency, so you will be tempted to behave in your old patterns that your mind is used to. It is important to resist this temptation as much as possible and continue to take the actions necessary to carry your subconscious mind to a better place.

Reality #3 – Change is Like Building Mental Muscle

If you have ever spent any time at the gym trying to get in shape, you know how long it takes to lose body fat and build lean muscle. However, if you exercise regularly for a long enough period of time, you can create a physique which is strikingly beautiful. The filmmaker Woody Allen once said that "80% of life is just showing up." This is certainly true with building a better body. The single biggest factor in changing your physical appearance is just showing up to work out.

This is also true with building a healthier subconscious mind. You have to think about your perceptions and emotions as mental muscle. You can build your mental muscle to create phenomenal mental health, but you have to do it by showing up and doing the exercises necessary to make it happen. Persistence is one of the keys to success.

Reality #4 – You are Defined by Your Surroundings

We have talked about the fact that the subconscious mind cannot differentiate self from non-self. Because of this, one of the realities of changing your emotions is that you must surround yourself with people who have the happiness and success you want. The actions and behavior of others is perceived by the subconscious, and this in turn stimulates emotional reactions and recalls emotional memories as though they were your actions and behaviors; just not as strongly as if you had done them yourself. This is why people pick up each other's habits when they spend a lot of time together. This is one of the major forces behind peer pressure and social conformity. If you want to lose weight and stop overeating, you will have better success by purposefully putting yourself in the company of people who look like you want to look. If you want to be happy, you will have better success by purposefully putting yourself in the company of people who feel the way you want to feel.

You can really accelerate your progress into a happier and more successful life by changing the people with whom you spend your time. This may seem kind of self-centered and unfair toward others with whom you may spend time now; like you are being a snob. What I would offer you is this thought: Ultimately your success in creating a very happy and fulfilling life can serve as a model for many other people to follow. You can serve as a powerfully positive influence on those around you. But if you can't break free from your own bondage of negativity, you will have little to offer.

Reality #5 – You Can't Believe Everything You Think

In the last chapter you were introduced to the concept of automated thoughts and how they arise out of your subconscious perceptions. Because your subconscious perceptions may not be the best reflection of how you want to see yourself and your world, you cannot always trust the thoughts that are generated by them. This means that you should not be too convinced that your decisions are correct or that what you think is right. You need to remain open to the idea that you may be wrong. On the other hand, you should also not take the position that you are incapable of making any good choices. This is just not true.

What has worked for me is just to hold onto the belief that half of everything I think is probably wrong – I just don't know what half. It is important when you are thinking about something important tthat you share your thoughts with someone who may have another perspective. You don't need to take their opinion as gospel, but the more you can explore alternative ways of looking at things, the better your chances of making a good decision for yourself.

Reality #6 – Being Nuts does not Mean You're Bad

I used to earnestly believe that I was crazy and that just about everyone else was happy and well-adjusted. For years, I beat myself up mentally because I believed that I was somehow weird, different, defective or alone because I felt so bad all of the time and I had such a low opinion of myself. Over the years, I have made the happy discovery that just about everyone else is nuts too! I have come to realize that being nuts in no way makes you a bad person. How happy or depressed you are and whether you engage in self-destructive behaviors is largely just due to the condition of your subconscious perceptions. Since your subconscious perceptions for the most part were created during a period of your life when you had little control over your world, you had very little control over whether you would grow up to be nuts or not.

However, now that you have grown up, the responsibility for your insanity rests with you. *Although you weren't responsible for becoming nuts, you now have total control over whether you remain nuts.*

Reality #7 – A High Quality of Life is the Payoff

The payoff for doing all of the work and enduring the feelings of disorientation and stress you experience by change is a high quality of life. A high quality of life may or may not include expensive cars, a boat, a huge house, or even a family, but your life will be filled with happiness and meaning. One of the goals of emotional growth is to reach a point where you want what you have, rather than have what you want.

In today's society, in which we tend to define ourseves by what we own, what position we hold and how much power we have, it sounds almost blasphemous to assert that the focus on attaining these things is usually at the expense of achieving a high quality of life. But, these two things are not mutually exclusive. You can have both as long as you place your emotional health first and material wealth second.

Reality #8 – The Past does not Equal the Future

Just as your past emotions and behavior were largely the result of how your emotional memory loops developed, your future emotions and behavior will be determined largely by how your emotional memory loops develop from now on. If you decide to do nothing to change them, they will just continue in their self-reinforcing pattern. If your past pattern has been one of negative emotions and self-defeating behaviors, your future pattern will be just more of the same.

However, if you decide that you want to change your emotional memory loop to self-reinforce a much more positive emotional experience and self-reinforce more positive behaviors, your future can be very different from your past. There is no such thing as pre-determination. Your destiny is solely in the hands of the emotional memory loop you maintain. Because of this, you are in complete control over what happens in your future. All you need to do is change your emotional memory loop and you will bump your feelings, thoughts and actions to a whole new level.

The Four Techniques to Change Your Emotions

Technique #1 – Creatively Use Phantom Events

As you learned in the discussion about emotional memories, phantom events are those which have emotional content and a completely fabricated factual content. Although phantom events are not real, they feel real and will be treated by the subconscious as though they were real. Phantom events can be imagined conversations we have with other people, images of being applauded or attacked, or any other imagined situation which creates an emotional response.

Because a phantom event is a type of emotional memory, you can purposely create a phantom event to change the way you feel and to change what perceptions your emotional memory loop is reinforcing. For example, imagine as vividly as you can that you are surrounded by people who are shaking your hand, smiling at you and telling you how much they appreciate you. Imagine and feel the emotions you experience in this situation.

If you did this simple exercise earnestly, you felt a change in your emotional state. This change will likely linger for a short time before you go back to your old emotional memory loop and you once again feel how you felt before. Because your perceptions develop out of your emotional experiences, you can creatively use phantom events to change your perceptions. You can imagine your life the way you want it to be, you can imagine feeling the way you want to feel, and you can imagine acting in the way you want to act. Each time you do this, you change your perceptions, provided that you are able to simultaneously experience emotion.

Technique #2 – Take Purposeful Action

This technique is similar to the technique described above, but instead of creating imagined events, as in the technique above, you are creating real ones. Because your mind is always striving for consistency between your perceptions, your thoughts, your feelings and your actions, you can change your thoughts, feelings and perceptions simply by changing your actions. If you want to feel better about yourself, you can act as if you did feel good about yourself and it will help make it so. You may feel silly *acting* like you feel good about yourself, but it doesn't matter. As long as you keep acting, you will change.

For most of my life, I was very afraid of other people. One of the behaviors which was driven by this fear was that I could not bring myself to look people in the eye. I was so intimidated by people and so scared of what they might do to me that I could never muster the courage to look at them face to face.

When I eventually decided that I would take the risk and begin looking people in the eye when I talked to them, it scared me to death. I had to purposely act in a way which was contrary to my perceptions. But without taking that action, I would never have been able to overcome my perception that the world and its people were dangerous and hostile.

Over time my perceptions changed and I began to lose my fear of other people. A big part of the change was due to the fact that I was willing to act as though people were nothing to fear and that they liked me. Taking purposeful action to change your perceptions is the simplest, but usually one of the scariest, techniques you can use to change your life.

Technique #3 – Imagine what You Would Think

Although it would be virtually impossible to control every thought that went through your mind in a day, you can purposely change the subject matter of your thoughts when negative thoughts start to creep in. Since your mind is always striving for consistency between your thoughts, emotions, actions and behaviors, if you can change your thoughts so that they are consistent with how you want to become, it will accelerate your growth.

Changing your thoughts is difficult because your thoughts are largely a product of your emotional memory loop, rather than a contributor of your emotional memory loop. However, you are more aware of your conscious thoughts than you are of your subconscious perceptions, or even what emotions you are experiencing, and changing your thoughts is a very effective way to help change your perceptions and emotions.

Technique #4 – Schmooze Your Way to Happiness

As you read in Reality #4, your subconscious mind cannot differentiate between self and non-self, so it is very important that you surround yourself with people who have the happiness and success that you want for yourself. The old saying "Tell me who your friends are and I'll tell you who you are" is very true. This is because how people around you react to different situations, the decisions they make, the things they talk about, the emotions they experience, are all things which you will pick up through empathy. Over time, those things will cause you to change. You will begin to think, feel and act the way in which the people around you do.

An example of how simply being around other people will lead to change in how you think, feel and act is related by Dr. Geri-Ann Galanti, a researcher and educator on cults and mind-control. Dr. Galanti went undercover to a Unification Church (The Moonie Cult) weekend retreat in 1983 to Camp K; a Moonie training camp in Northern California. She writes:

"One by one, my expectations of the appearance of overt mind control crumbled. Not only did they present themselves openly as Moonies and look "normal," but also once we were up at the camp I experienced no lack of sleep, protein deprivation, or badgering. Both mornings I arose around 8:30 or 9:00 – when I got tired of lying around; there was no telling me to get up early. We were fed eggs, fish, tuna, cheese, and other protein-rich foods during the three daily meals, plus there were three snacks each day. I was "allowed" to talk privately – if only briefly – with other new recruits;

I even had occasional moments to myself. Where was all this so-called brainwashing?

"During the three doctrinal lectures per day, each lasting about an hour to an hour and a half, I sat smugly critiquing the lectures to myself. Seven years in graduate school, plus a year in the School of Education, prepared me well for this task. I amused myself by noting the kinds of techniques they utilized.

"Because of my education and background, I was far more prepared than the average recruit to deal with the influence process. Psychologically I was protected by a very strong belief system of my own, as well as by my self-imposed role as observer. At no time did I feel that my beliefs were being influenced; my intellect appeared intact. I was actively monitoring myself the entire weekend. The fact that despite all this I was *influenced underscores the power of the techniques of persuasion.*

"I was beginning to act like them: cheering wildly at mediocre performances, reporting attitudes that I felt would meet with their approval, actively participating in games and songs from childhood. My attitudes were also changing. Most telling was a remark I made to the friend I had arranged to pick me up from Camp K: "I had a great time. Remind me again what's so bad about the Moonies."

"The day after the camp experience I was interviewing a former deprogrammer who had spent several years in the Moonies. About halfway through the interview I asked her to describe exactly what she did during a deprogramming. She looked me straight in the eye and said, 'Exactly what I've been doing with you.'"

(Exerpt from: Recovery From Cults: Help For Victims of Psychological and Spiritual Abuse. Edited by: Michael Langone)

This story illustrates the power that the people around us have on our thoughts and behavior. The technique of changing your behavior by surrounding yourself with healthy people takes advantage of the fact that your subconscious mind cannot differentiate self from non-self.

To Sum Up About Three Facts, Eight Realities and Four Techniques

In this chapter you learned about the fact that your subconscious mind is always striving for consistency between your perceptions, emotions, thoughts and actions. You learned that the subconscious mind cannot differentiate between real or imagined events, nor can it differentiate between self and non-self. This means that you can respond emotionally to events which are not real and don't even involve you.

You learned a number of realities about change, including the reality that you will experience disorientation any time you change, and that being a little nuts is not something to feel bad about. You also learned four important techniques which are effective in changing your perceptions, emotions, thoughts and behavior, by changing your emotional memory loop: using phantom events, taking purposeful action, redirecting your thoughts, and surrounding yourself with healthy people.

In the exercise that follows, you will learn how you can apply all of these things on a daily basis by using a simple *Daily Perception Diary*.

Exercise

The Daily Perception Diary

~~~~~~~~~~~~~~~~~~

    Now comes the fun part; the time when you can take all of the theory and techniques you learned in the previous chapters and put them into action. The Daily Perception Diary is designed to help you do three major things. First, it will help you develop a better awareness of your emotions and how they affect your behavior. Second, it will help you develop healthier responses to emotional situations. Third, it will help you track your progress from week-to-week, and if you decide to continue doing the exercise it will help you track your progress from month-to-month, or year-to-year. It is very encouraging when you can look back at the feelings you struggled with several months ago and realize that you no longer struggle with them.

    This diary is set up so that each day you work through a quick exercise. It is probably best done at night because the events and feelings of the day are still fresh in your mind. An example is filled out for you on the next page.

The Daily Perception Diary - Example

Emotional Event: _I had an argument with my partner. I found out she lied to me._

Secondary Emotion: _I felt angry and hurt._

Primary Emotion: ☒ Fear ☐ Stress ☐ Anxiety ☒ Worthlessness
☐ Attraction ☐ Confidence ☐ Empowerment ☐ Joy

Actions I Took: _I confronted her about lying to me._

Results: _We began to fight and now we both feel very upset._

What I Could Do Different Next Time: _I could ask her what made her feel like she had to lie to me instead of just jumping on her for lying to me._

Phantom Event: _When I was driving to work today, this vision of being involved in an accident kept going through my head._

Automatic Thought: _I kept thinking that nobody liked me. I kept trying to over-analyse what everyone was saying._

My Evaluation of My Day: _The fight was a fitting end to kind of a bad day. One thing I noticed is that all of my emotional stuff today revolved around my low perception of value - except for the fear of an accident. Tomorrow, I will talk to my partner to try to see if there was something I was doing to make her want to lie to me._

The Daily Perception Diary - Day 1

Emotional Event: _____

Secondary Emotion: _____

Primary Emotion: ☐ Fear   ☐ Stress   ☐ Anxiety   ☐ Worthlessness
                  ☐ Attraction   ☐ Confidence   ☐ Empowerment   ☐ Joy

Actions I Took: _____

Results: _____

What I Could Do Different Next Time: _____
_____

Phantom Event: _____
_____

Automatic Thought: _____
_____

My Evaluation of My Day: _____
_____
_____
_____

The Daily Perception Diary - Day 2

Emotional Event: _____

Secondary Emotion: _____

Primary Emotion: ☐ Fear ☐ Stress ☐ Anxiety ☐ Worthlessness
                  ☐ Attraction ☐ Confidence ☐ Empowerment ☐ Joy

Actions I Took: _____

Results: _____

What I Could Do Different Next Time: _____
_____

Phantom Event: _____
_____

Automatic Thought: _____
_____

My Evaluation of My Day: _____
_____
_____
_____

The Daily Perception Diary - Day 3

Emotional Event: _____

Secondary Emotion: _____

Primary Emotion: ☐ Fear ☐ Stress ☐ Anxiety ☐ Worthlessness
☐ Attraction ☐ Confidence ☐ Empowerment ☐ Joy

Actions I Took: _____

Results: _____

What I Could Do Different Next Time: _____
_____

Phantom Event: _____
_____

Automatic Thought: _____
_____

My Evaluation of My Day: _____
_____
_____

The Daily Perception Diary - Day 4

Emotional Event: _____

Secondary Emotion: _____

Primary Emotion: ☐ Fear ☐ Stress ☐ Anxiety ☐ Worthlessness
 ☐ Attraction ☐ Confidence ☐ Empowerment ☐ Joy

Actions I Took: _____

Results: _____

What I Could Do Different Next Time: _____

_____

Phantom Event: _____

_____

Automatic Thought: _____

_____

My Evaluation of My Day: _____

_____

_____

_____

The Daily Perception Diary - Day 5

Emotional Event: _____

Secondary Emotion: _____

Primary Emotion: ☐ Fear   ☐ Stress   ☐ Anxiety   ☐ Worthlessness
                  ☐ Attraction   ☐ Confidence   ☐ Empowerment   ☐ Joy

Actions I Took: _____

Results: _____

What I Could Do Different Next Time: _____
_____

Phantom Event: _____
_____

Automatic Thought: _____
_____

My Evaluation of My Day: _____
_____
_____
_____

The Daily Perception Diary - Day 6

Emotional Event: _____

Secondary Emotion: _____

Primary Emotion: ☐ Fear   ☐ Stress   ☐ Anxiety   ☐ Worthlessness
                  ☐ Attraction   ☐ Confidence   ☐ Empowerment   ☐ Joy

Actions I Took: _____

Results: _____

What I Could Do Different Next Time: _____
_____

Phantom Event: _____
_____

Automatic Thought: _____
_____

My Evaluation of My Day: _____
_____
_____
_____

The Daily Perception Diary - Day 7

Emotional Event: _____

Secondary Emotion: _____

Primary Emotion: ☐ Fear   ☐ Stress   ☐ Anxiety   ☐ Worthlessness
                  ☐ Attraction   ☐ Confidence   ☐ Empowerment   ☐ Joy

Actions I Took: _____

Results: _____

What I Could Do Different Next Time: _____

_____

Phantom Event: _____

_____

Automatic Thought: _____

_____

My Evaluation of My Day: _____

_____

_____

The Daily Perception Diary - Day 8

Emotional Event: _____

Secondary Emotion: _____

Primary Emotion: ☐ Fear   ☐ Stress   ☐ Anxiety   ☐ Worthlessness
　　　　　　　　　☐ Attraction   ☐ Confidence   ☐ Empowerment   ☐ Joy

Actions I Took: _____

Results: _____

What I Could Do Different Next Time: _____

_____

Phantom Event: _____

_____

Automatic Thought: _____

_____

My Evaluation of My Day: _____

_____

_____

The Daily Perception Diary - Day 9

Emotional Event: _____

Secondary Emotion: _____

Primary Emotion: ☐ Fear ☐ Stress ☐ Anxiety ☐ Worthlessness
                  ☐ Attraction ☐ Confidence ☐ Empowerment ☐ Joy

Actions I Took: _____

Results: _____

What I Could Do Different Next Time: _____

_____

Phantom Event: _____

_____

Automatic Thought: _____

_____

My Evaluation of My Day: _____

_____

_____

The Daily Perception Diary - Day 10

Emotional Event: _____

Secondary Emotion: _____

Primary Emotion: ☐ Fear   ☐ Stress   ☐ Anxiety   ☐ Worthlessness
                  ☐ Attraction   ☐ Confidence   ☐ Empowerment   ☐ Joy

Actions I Took: _____

Results: _____

What I Could Do Different Next Time: _____
_____

Phantom Event: _____
_____

Automatic Thought: _____
_____

My Evaluation of My Day: _____
_____
_____
_____

The Daily Perception Diary - Day 11

Emotional Event: _____

Secondary Emotion: _____

Primary Emotion: ☐ Fear   ☐ Stress   ☐ Anxiety   ☐ Worthlessness
                   ☐ Attraction   ☐ Confidence   ☐ Empowerment   ☐ Joy

Actions I Took: _____

Results: _____

What I Could Do Different Next Time: _____

_____

Phantom Event: _____

_____

Automatic Thought: _____

_____

My Evaluation of My Day: _____

_____

_____

The Daily Perception Diary - Day 12

Emotional Event: _____

Secondary Emotion: _____

Primary Emotion: ☐ Fear   ☐ Stress   ☐ Anxiety   ☐ Worthlessness
               ☐ Attraction   ☐ Confidence   ☐ Empowerment   ☐ Joy

Actions I Took: _____

Results: _____

What I Could Do Different Next Time: _____

_____

Phantom Event: _____

_____

Automatic Thought: _____

_____

My Evaluation of My Day: _____

_____

_____

_____

The Daily Perception Diary - Day 13

Emotional Event: _____

Secondary Emotion: _____

Primary Emotion: ☐ Fear   ☐ Stress   ☐ Anxiety   ☐ Worthlessness
               ☐ Attraction   ☐ Confidence   ☐ Empowerment   ☐ Joy

Actions I Took: _____

Results: _____

What I Could Do Different Next Time: _____
_____

Phantom Event: _____
_____

Automatic Thought: _____
_____

My Evaluation of My Day: _____
_____
_____
_____

The Daily Perception Diary - Day 14

Emotional Event: _____

Secondary Emotion: _____

Primary Emotion: ☐ Fear   ☐ Stress   ☐ Anxiety   ☐ Worthlessness
                  ☐ Attraction   ☐ Confidence   ☐ Empowerment   ☐ Joy

Actions I Took: _____

Results: _____

What I Could Do Different Next Time: _____

_____

Phantom Event: _____

_____

Automatic Thought: _____

_____

My Evaluation of My Day: _____

_____

_____

The Daily Perception Diary - Day 15

Emotional Event: _____

Secondary Emotion: _____

Primary Emotion: ☐ Fear ☐ Stress ☐ Anxiety ☐ Worthlessness
 ☐ Attraction ☐ Confidence ☐ Empowerment ☐ Joy

Actions I Took: _____

Results: _____

What I Could Do Different Next Time: _____

_____

Phantom Event: _____

_____

Automatic Thought: _____

_____

My Evaluation of My Day: _____

_____

_____

The Daily Perception Diary - Day 16

Emotional Event: _____

Secondary Emotion: _____

Primary Emotion: ☐ Fear   ☐ Stress   ☐ Anxiety   ☐ Worthlessness
                  ☐ Attraction   ☐ Confidence   ☐ Empowerment   ☐ Joy

Actions I Took: _____

Results: _____

What I Could Do Different Next Time: _____

_____

Phantom Event: _____

_____

Automatic Thought: _____

_____

My Evaluation of My Day: _____

_____

_____

The Daily Perception Diary - Day 17

Emotional Event: _____

Secondary Emotion: _____

Primary Emotion: ☐ Fear   ☐ Stress   ☐ Anxiety   ☐ Worthlessness
                  ☐ Attraction   ☐ Confidence   ☐ Empowerment   ☐ Joy

Actions I Took: _____

Results: _____

What I Could Do Different Next Time: _____
_____

Phantom Event: _____
_____

Automatic Thought: _____
_____

My Evaluation of My Day: _____
_____
_____

The Daily Perception Diary - Day 18

Emotional Event: _____

Secondary Emotion: _____

Primary Emotion: ☐ Fear   ☐ Stress   ☐ Anxiety   ☐ Worthlessness
 ☐ Attraction   ☐ Confidence   ☐ Empowerment   ☐ Joy

Actions I Took: _____

Results: _____

What I Could Do Different Next Time: _____

_____

Phantom Event: _____

_____

Automatic Thought: _____

_____

My Evaluation of My Day: _____

_____

_____

The Daily Perception Diary - Day 19

Emotional Event: _____

Secondary Emotion: _____

Primary Emotion: ☐ Fear   ☐ Stress   ☐ Anxiety   ☐ Worthlessness
                  ☐ Attraction   ☐ Confidence   ☐ Empowerment   ☐ Joy

Actions I Took: _____

Results: _____

What I Could Do Different Next Time: _____
_____

Phantom Event: _____
_____

Automatic Thought: _____
_____

My Evaluation of My Day: _____
_____
_____

The Daily Perception Diary - Day 20

Emotional Event: _____

Secondary Emotion: _____

Primary Emotion: ☐ Fear   ☐ Stress   ☐ Anxiety   ☐ Worthlessness
                  ☐ Attraction ☐ Confidence ☐ Empowerment ☐ Joy

Actions I Took: _____

Results: _____

What I Could Do Different Next Time: _____
_____

Phantom Event: _____
_____

Automatic Thought: _____
_____

My Evaluation of My Day: _____
_____
_____
_____

The Daily Perception Diary - Day 21

Emotional Event: _____

Secondary Emotion: _____

Primary Emotion: ☐ Fear   ☐ Stress   ☐ Anxiety   ☐ Worthlessness
          ☐ Attraction   ☐ Confidence   ☐ Empowerment   ☐ Joy

Actions I Took: _____

Results: _____

What I Could Do Different Next Time: _____
_____

Phantom Event: _____
_____

Automatic Thought: _____
_____

My Evaluation of My Day: _____
_____
_____

The Daily Perception Diary - Day 22

Emotional Event: _____

Secondary Emotion: _____

Primary Emotion: ☐ Fear ☐ Stress ☐ Anxiety ☐ Worthlessness
    ☐ Attraction ☐ Confidence ☐ Empowerment ☐ Joy

Actions I Took: _____

Results: _____

What I Could Do Different Next Time: _____

_____

Phantom Event: _____

_____

Automatic Thought: _____

_____

My Evaluation of My Day: _____

_____

_____

_____

The Daily Perception Diary - Day 23

Emotional Event: _____

Secondary Emotion: _____

Primary Emotion: ☐ Fear   ☐ Stress   ☐ Anxiety   ☐ Worthlessness
            ☐ Attraction   ☐ Confidence   ☐ Empowerment   ☐ Joy

Actions I Took: _____

Results: _____

What I Could Do Different Next Time: _____

_____

Phantom Event: _____

_____

Automatic Thought: _____

_____

My Evaluation of My Day: _____

_____

_____

The Daily Perception Diary - Day 24

Emotional Event: _____

Secondary Emotion: _____

Primary Emotion: ☐ Fear   ☐ Stress   ☐ Anxiety   ☐ Worthlessness
          ☐ Attraction   ☐ Confidence   ☐ Empowerment   ☐ Joy

Actions I Took: _____

Results: _____

What I Could Do Different Next Time: _____

_____

Phantom Event: _____

_____

Automatic Thought: _____

_____

My Evaluation of My Day: _____

_____

_____

_____

The Daily Perception Diary - Day 25

Emotional Event: _____

Secondary Emotion: _____

Primary Emotion: ☐ Fear ☐ Stress ☐ Anxiety ☐ Worthlessness
  ☐ Attraction ☐ Confidence ☐ Empowerment ☐ Joy

Actions I Took: _____

Results: _____

What I Could Do Different Next Time: _____
_____

Phantom Event: _____
_____

Automatic Thought: _____
_____

My Evaluation of My Day: _____
_____
_____
_____

The Daily Perception Diary - Day 26

Emotional Event: _____

Secondary Emotion: _____

Primary Emotion: ☐ Fear   ☐ Stress   ☐ Anxiety   ☐ Worthlessness
                  ☐ Attraction   ☐ Confidence   ☐ Empowerment   ☐ Joy

Actions I Took: _____

Results: _____

What I Could Do Different Next Time: _____

_____

Phantom Event: _____

_____

Automatic Thought: _____

_____

My Evaluation of My Day: _____

_____

_____

The Daily Perception Diary - Day 27

Emotional Event: _____

Secondary Emotion: _____

Primary Emotion: ☐ Fear   ☐ Stress   ☐ Anxiety   ☐ Worthlessness
                  ☐ Attraction   ☐ Confidence   ☐ Empowerment   ☐ Joy

Actions I Took: _____

Results: _____

What I Could Do Different Next Time: _____
_____

Phantom Event: _____
_____

Automatic Thought: _____
_____

My Evaluation of My Day: _____
_____
_____
_____

The Daily Perception Diary - Day 28

Emotional Event: _____

Secondary Emotion: _____

Primary Emotion: ☐ Fear ☐ Stress ☐ Anxiety ☐ Worthlessness
☐ Attraction ☐ Confidence ☐ Empowerment ☐ Joy

Actions I Took: _____

Results: _____

What I Could Do Different Next Time: _____

_____

Phantom Event: _____

_____

Automatic Thought: _____

_____

My Evaluation of My Day: _____

_____

_____

The Daily Perception Diary - Day 29

Emotional Event: _____

Secondary Emotion: _____

Primary Emotion: ☐ Fear   ☐ Stress   ☐ Anxiety   ☐ Worthlessness
                  ☐ Attraction   ☐ Confidence   ☐ Empowerment   ☐ Joy

Actions I Took: _____

Results: _____

What I Could Do Different Next Time: _____
_____

Phantom Event: _____
_____

Automatic Thought: _____
_____

My Evaluation of My Day: _____
_____
_____

The Daily Perception Diary - Day 30

Emotional Event: _____

Secondary Emotion: _____

Primary Emotion: ☐ Fear   ☐ Stress   ☐ Anxiety   ☐ Worthlessness
                   ☐ Attraction   ☐ Confidence   ☐ Empowerment   ☐ Joy

Actions I Took: _____

Results: _____

What I Could Do Different Next Time: _____
_____

Phantom Event: _____
_____

Automatic Thought: _____
_____

My Evaluation of My Day: _____
_____
_____
_____

Glossary

Anxiety – The primary emotion elicited when we perceive that we have no control over the events in our environment. Anxiety is one of the emotions which will stimulate the "fight, flight or freeze" response. Anxiety is the opposite emotion to empowerment.

Attraction – The primary emotion elicited when we perceive that the world around us is nurturing. This emotion is responsible for bonding and intimacy within relationships. Attraction is the opposite emotion to fear.

Automatic Thoughts – These are fragments of conversations, images and situations which fill our consciousness throughout the day. They result from the recollection of emotional memories.

Confidence – The primary emotion experienced when we have the perception that our environment is very predictable; that we know what is going to happen. Confidence is the opposite emotion to stress.

Conscious Mind – The part of our mental processing which makes up our awareness. All of our beliefs, problem-solving abilities and factual memories reside in the conscious mind.

Effectiveness – The subconscious perception about our ability to handle challenges we face or about our ability to control our environment. The perception of effectiveness will stimulate two emotions: the positive emotion of empowerment and the negative emotion of anxiety.

Emotion – A short-duration, high-intensity, rapid-onset change in our feelings, often coupled with physiological changes, such as elevated blood pressure, depending on the emotion experienced. Emotions are a primitive and powerful survival mechanism.

Emotional Centers – There are two centers in a structure of the brain called the amygdala which, are responsible for generating emotions. One center stimulates the generation of positive emotions, one center stimulates the generation of negative emotions.

Perceptive Filter – A term given to the phenomenon which controls our reaction to events as we perceive them. In this way, our perceptions become a filter which creates the tendency to respond to all events in a similar and predictable fashion.

Emotional Hijacking – Occurs when emotions become so overwhelming that they take control of our actions, causing us to act in ways that defy our self-will, such as addictive behavior, tantrums or rage.

Emotional Memory – A two-part memory of an event comprised of an emotional component and a factual component. The emotional component is stored in the subconscious mind, whereas the factual component is stored in the conscious mind. When we experience an emotion, our subconscious recalls emotional memories that have a similar emotional content.

Emotional Memory Loop – A multi-stage phenomenon whereby our perceptions are reinforced by emotional memories. An emotional response to an event triggers the recall of an emotional memory. When that emotional memory is re-experienced, it stimulates the recall of another emotional memory. This forms a loop by which perceptions, emotions and emotional memories reinforce each other.

Empowerment – The primary emotion elicited when you have the perception that you can effectively navigate the obstacles and overcome the challenges you face. Empowerment is the opposite emotion to anxiety.

Fear – The primary emotion experienced when there is a perceived danger or threat. Fear is an emotion which will stimulate the "fight, flight or freeze" response. Fear is the opposite emotion to attraction.

Feelings – Affective states which include the primary and secondary emotions, as well as the non-emotional states, such as being tired, alert, or curious.

Hostility – The subconscious perception about how hostile or nurturing our environment is. This perception will stimulate the positive emotion of attraction or the negative emotion of fear.

Joy – The primary emotion elicited whenever we have the perception that we are valued by others. Joy is the emotion responsible for allowing us to experience meaning in our life. Joy is the opposite emotion to worthlessness.

Mood – The experience created by the emotional memory loop. If the emotional memory loop causes us to re-experience negative emotions, we will be "in a bad mood." If the emotional memory loop replays positive emotions, we will be "in a good mood." Mood is simply the pattern of emotions experienced.

Perception – The subconscious process of interpreting the meaning in the events we experience about ourselves and the world around us. There are a total of four subconscious perceptions – value, effectiveness, predictability and hostility – which are responsible for generating primary and secondary emotions, and which develop in early childhood.

Phantom Event – A phenomenon where our conscious mind creates a scenario to take the place of the degraded factual portion of an emotional memory. Because this fabricated scenario is attached to an emotion, we experience the phantom event as though it were a real event.

Predictability – The subconscious perception about how structured or chaotic our world is. This perception is responsible for stimulating the positive emotion of confidence or the negative emotion of stress.

Primary Emotions – Emotions which are stimulated by our subconscious perceptions. They are hard-wired responses and require no conscious processing to be experienced; for example, fear or stress.

Secondary Emotions – Emotional responses which require conscious processing in order to be experienced, such as anger. They are comprised of one or a mixture primary emotions together with a conscious interpretation.

Sensitivity – The intensity with which we experience emotions and sensory stimulation. A person with a high-sensitivity temperament is someone who experiences emotions very intensely, whereas a person with a low-sensitivity temperament is someone who experiences very subtle emotions.

Stress – One of the primary emotions that is stimulated whenever there is a perception of a loss of predictability in one's life. Any life change, good or bad, will stimulate this emotion. Stress is the opposite emotion to confidence.

Subconscious Mind – The part of our mental processing which takes place below the level of our awareness. Its roles in emotion are housing our perceptions, and storing emotional and procedural memory.

Temperament – The part of our mental processing which is biologically hard-wired mental functions, such as sensitivity. These aspects of our personality do not change appreciably throughout life.

Value – The perception of how important we are to people around us. This perception will generate either the positive emotion of joy, or the negative emotion of worthlessness.

Worthlessness – The primary emotion experienced whenever there is the perception that we are not valued by those around us, and often leads to depression. Worthlessness is the opposite emotion to joy.

Index

action 109, 114-115
anger 2, 46
anxiety 2, 24, 37-39
apathy 47
Asche, S.E. 39
attention deficit disorder 57-58
attraction 26-27, 42-44
automatic thoughts 83, 85-87, 115-116
behavior 3, 87-89, 93, 109
   proactive 3, 93, 109
   reactive 3, 87-89
Burns, David 85
change 13, 14, 40, 41-42, 107-109, 110, 113-117
Cobain, Kurt 19-20
cognitive distortions 84
confidence 25, 39-42

conformity 39-40, 110-111, 116-117
consistency 91-92, 106-107
cults 116-117
daily perception diary 118, 119-150
Dalai Lama 20
decisions 87-89
depression 2, 36, 84
desperation 2, 46
disappointment 47
disorientation 107-109
effectiveness 23-24, 37-39
emotions 3, 4, 20-49
   awareness 48
   primary 4, 35-44
   secondary 4, 44-49
   vs. feelings 28-29
emotional bondage 89-90

emotional centers 34-35
emotional hijacking 7-8, 12, 62-64
emotional intensity 6, 57-66
emotional memories 8-11, 73-94
emotional memory loop 8-11, 73-94
empowerment 24, 37-39
exercise 14
factual memory 74
fear 2, 26-27, 42-44
feelings 28-29
Frankl Viktor 36
Fromm, Erich 42
Galanti, Geri-Ann 116-117
guarding 47
hostility 26-27, 42-44
joy 23, 36-37
logotherapy 36
Miller, David 57-58
mood 82-83
Moonies 116-117
nurturing 26-27

nuts 112
perceptions 4, 21-27, 29-49, 90-93
perceptive filter 30-34
phantom events 78-80, 92-93, 113-114
predictability 25-26, 39-42
procedural memory 74-75
quality of life 112-113
rage 46
relationships 3, 65-66
sensitivity 6-7, 57-66
   genetics 60-62
   high-sensitivity 6-7, 62-65
   low-sensitivity 6-7
self-fulfilling prophecy 11-12
stress 2, 25-26, 39-42
subconscious 20-49, 103-107
survival 3, 21-27
temperament 57-58
value 22-23, 36
withdrawal 46
worthlessness 23, 36-37

Dr. Todd

For most of Dr. Todd's adult life, he has sought to answer three questions. First, what drives people to act in ways that undermines their happiness and success in life; even when they know better? Second, why is it that some individuals are able to overcome tremendous obstacles in their lives, while others continue to struggle? Third, what simple key elements, if applied, will lead to an improved quality of life?

The techniques and information which Dr. Todd has developed over the past couple of decades have allowed him to grow from being a functionally illiterate drug addict living in an abandoned house to being a successful husband, doctor, author and professional speaker. His experience, insights and information have helped numerous people transform their lives.

Speaking in a dynamic and articulate style, he has the rare ability to communicate complex ideas in a way that anyone can understand them. His dedication to help others through his writing and speaking, together with his craving for truth and a passionate optimism for humanity, earns him the title of a truly "Hyperactive Overeducated Visionary."

Dr. Todd is available to present to your business group, conference or workshop. Custom programs are available. Contact Dr. Todd via the web or e-mail at:

Web site: www.drtodd.com
E-Mail: drtodd@drtodd.com

Printed in the United States
882700001B